LOVE SONG FOR HAITI
A MEMOIR OF LIFE WITH STREET BOYS

CHARLOTTE ONEILLE ADAMS

ALSO BY CHARLOTTE ONEILLE ADAMS

An Unexpected Passion

The Rose and the Blade

A Fish Feast

ISBN 978-0-578-78173-0

Copyright © pending 2020 Charlotte Oneille Adams

Library of Congress Control Number: 2020923829

All rights reserved. No part of this book can be used or reproduced in any manner without written permission except in the context of reviews. To obtain permission, write to *WatershedStoryteller@gmail.com*

San Diego, California

This is a memoir, and as such, are the personal recollections and opinions of the author. For the protection of privacy, all names have been changed with the exception of the author's, her daughter's and a few public names.

The proverbs are derived from oral traditions in the collective community.

Fo ou bat tanbou-a, pou tande son-li.
"*You must beat the drum to hear its sound.*"

— HAITIAN PROVERB

CONTENTS

Map of Haiti	ix
Introduction	xi
Chapter 1	1
Chapter 2	13
Chapter 3	29
Chapter 4	43
Chapter 5	53
Chapter 6	69
Chapter 7	83
Chapter 8	95
Chapter 9	105
Chapter 10	117
Chapter 11	135
Chapter 12	145
Chapter 13	155
Chapter 14	163
Chapter 15	177
Chapter 16	189
Chapter 17	205
Chapter 18	213
Chapter 19	225
Chapter 20	233
Chapter 21	249
Chapter 22	259
Chapter 23	269
Epilogue	281

The ECHO Program	285
End.	293
L'HISTOIRE:	295
The Confluence	309
Acknowledgments	315
About the Author	319

For

Shelley

and the

timoun nan lari-yo of Petionville

MAP OF HAITI

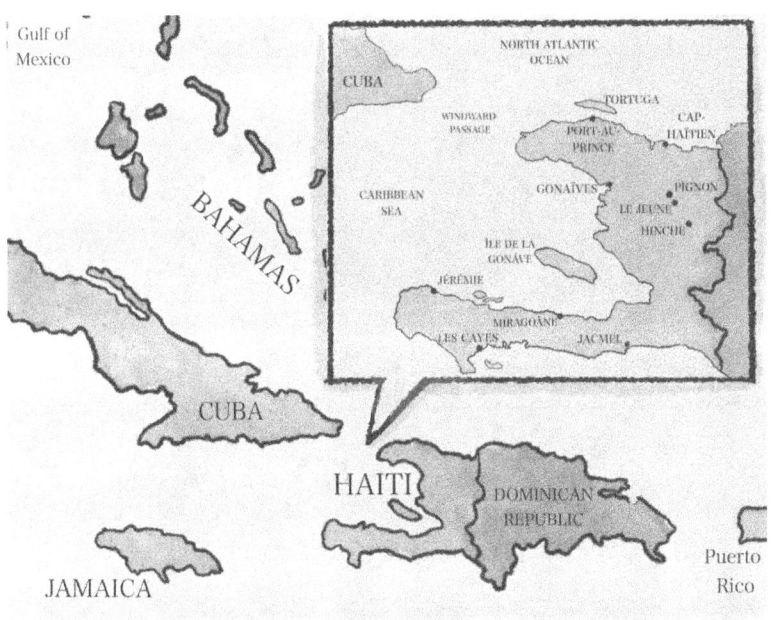

Map design by Melia Wright, July 2020

INTRODUCTION

I do not deny the blood that spilled in Haiti in 1993-1994, the turbulent years of the United Nations embargo leading to the American invasion in 1994. That is not what I choose to remember.

Even now, decades later, after the "event" in 2010 when the earthquake shattered all things frail, and after the hurricane devastation in 2016, the images I see are youthful eyes that sparkle with joy or pop with surprise. I see eyes with quiet yearnings or silent fears that beckon, like curtained doorways, to unheard songs of sweetness and pain.

If I concentrate, I hear a *bonjour* of greetings, endless banter and laughter, and, of course, wheedling and begging. That comes with street territory. A territory I refused to tread when I arrived in May of 1993.

CHAPTER ONE

"It is the tone that makes the music."

— FRENCH PROVERB

I stood alone on the steaming tarmac of the Port-au-Prince International Airport and squinted at a palm tree. Blips from training flipped through my mind like foreign language flash cards. Aggressive culture. Unpredictable. African *Vodou* roots. French colony, slave history.

Inside the baggage claim warehouse was chaos. At the conveyor belt, I turned at the tap on my shoulder.

"You must be Charlotte Wright." Extending his hand, he

said, "I'm Hans Jansen. I convinced the customs official you might need a hand."

I was replacing Hans as the Field Director in Haiti for an international Christian nonprofit organization that focused on development in poor countries. Working on the front line, usually in the back country, they worked with the poorest of the population.

When we exited, Hans emphatically rejected efforts of grown men reaching for my bags. Approaching the parking lot, I audibly sighed.

"Don't relax too soon." Smiling as though he might share a secret, Hans nodded toward a chain link fence.

I looked at the almost empty parking lot where a group of survivors operated, around fifteen teenage boys.

When they saw us, they picked up speed, like a herd of wildebeests galloping across an asphalt plain. A vehicle entered the area, and part of the herd veered to meet the new arrivals. The remainder surrounded us with knotty knees under cut-off shorts and ill-fitting, worn tennis shoes.

I froze.

Fierce tugs-of-war broke out over my luggage, and Hans

lost his grasp on the handle. Helplessly, I watched two boys pull my suitcase in opposite directions.

"It's going to rip apart," I said to no one, for Hans had left the suitcase dispute. Marching on, he was well on his way to the SUV.

"Stop!" I shouted at the boys.

At the moment I reached to intervene, the larger boy prevailed. Looking at me, he tapped his chest proclaiming victory and then hustled to follow Hans, my bag in tow.

Trailing behind, I warily scrutinized several boys surrounding me. In their late teens, they had a beaten-about-the-world look of scruffy toughness and a single goal manifested in outstretched hands.

"A little something, Madame."

Striding beside me, their expectant, dirty hands entreated me to hand over my shoulder bag.

I shook my head and continued walking toward the SUV.

When a bold one jerked the shoulder strap, I clutched the bag to my body and shouted, "NO!" My narrowed eyes told the boy I meant business. He backed away.

Meanwhile, the victor of the tug-of-war placed my suitcase

in the rear of the SUV and extended his palm toward Hans for payment.

In fact, all of the boys demanded payment. With hands casually cocked on their hips or their index fingers resting astride their noses, they named their price.

"A little something."

Ignoring them, Hans took my shoulder bag and arranged it in the rear. When I opened my purse to tip the victor, Hans quickly placed his hand over it.

"Don't do that."

Outraged at the interruption of their payment, the boys shouted in an angry dialect. Arms flailing, their circle closed around us.

My eyes widened.

Although severely outnumbered, Hans ignored their badgering. He calmly looked at me and said, "Never give money to beggars."

Just like that. As though they weren't there, a perfect disconnect. We might as well have been in a parallel universe, and the ruffians, invisible.

Nonchalantly, Hans closed the rear door and walked through the boys toward the driver's side.

I looked into the face of an older boy. He shrugged as if to say *c'est la vie* and galloped off to join others who had encircled another car.

A truck taxi called a tap-tap

As we pulled from the lot into traffic, Hans said, "Here's some advice. If you give, you're on the hook. Not only does the beggar you gave money to return, but his friends and family, or whoever, come, too. Trust me. Establish your reputation early, Charlotte. Don't give."

From the airport road, we turned on a main artery polluted with traffic and dust. Hans turned up the air conditioner.

"Here's the truth about the begging," he continued. "They

make *you* responsible for solving their problems, and the solution is always *your money*."

He tapped the steering wheel twice in time with "your money."

"That's not good. Still, I don't know if I can look the other way."

"That's exactly what you have to do. Never make eye contact and never give. Set your boundaries. You'll be all right.""

Unsettled about the parking lot experience, I asked, "What about those boys? Who are they?"

"The *timoun nan lari-yo* are the worst. That literally translates as "children of the street," and it refers to children without mamas. You'll encounter them everywhere, that group in the parking lot, at grocery stores, always at Lynx Air Office where we get our mail. They hang out there for the internationals. That's where we're going now, by the way."

Hans droned on about the street boys. I learned that in the Kreyol language, the phrase "children without mamas" infers they have no morality or values, the lowest of the low, capable of committing any act. They are the bottom of the bottom.

Honestly, I wasn't paying serious attention. I was more interested in diversions outside the car window.

I wanted to look into those steaming black cauldrons propped over charcoal fires and inhale the aromas. I wanted to listen to women's foreign voices as they stirred their cauldrons or hawked their breads and vegetables.

I drank it all in. Shirtless construction workers balanced on wobbling scaffolding made from tree sticks. "Tree sticks, for goodness' sake! Imagine that."

Women in silk bargained with women merchants sitting on the ground or walking with baskets on their heads. In every hue of skin color and in every class of dress, pedestrians filled the walks and streets.

Every scene pulsed with life, and I felt my own life pulse rise and resonate with those rhythms. *Haiti is raw energy.*

"We're climbing, aren't we? I like the full trees."

"We're almost to Petionville, the area where most internationals live. Less dust and congestion. Good French restaurants, a grocery store. Presse Evangelique is up here, too, down that shaded street. You'll take Kreyol lessons there."

"Can I find a house in this area?"

"Probably."

"Where do you attend church?"

"We go to the Episcopal near here. The missionaries attend a larger church that has a school, but much further away. Their children attend that school. There's another English-speaking service nearby in a private home of a retired pastor. I hear that's good."

I nodded.

"Why did you come to Haiti, Charlotte? I heard you were a top realtor. A Christian nonprofit in Haiti is a far cry from that lifestyle."

My tongue played with my teeth while I considered what to share. It was complicated. I chose the basic truth.

"Real estate was good, but it didn't fill my heart. I felt God calling me to do something else. I wanted to do development work, but I was busy with my family. This opportunity presented itself. I was qualified, and so I'm here."

Hans half-smiled.

"So, you came to change Haiti." He looked at me for a moment. "You'll never change Haiti, Charlotte, but Haiti will change you."

I was contemplating that insight when Hans suddenly

whipped into a parking space at Lynx Air Office and popped open his door. "The office is up those stairs," he said, pointing to an exterior staircase to a second story. "Mail comes in daily around noon. Come on."

I turned to a crescendo of tapping on my window.

Four street boys bent, their faces staring against the glass, motioning for me to roll down the window. I looked up the stairs after Hans, but he was not to be seen.

I studied the boys through the window. Younger than the airport gang, they were more like thirteen, and a youthful innocence in their bright eyes.

The moment I opened the car door, the boys crowded, clamoring for "a little something, pleez, Madame."

"I don't speak Kreyol," I muttered, pushing through them.

Like flies on ripe fruit, they moved with me as I went forward, and newcomers joined the buzzing encirclement. Boys pushed each other aside as each tried to get closer and whisper his personal plight in my ear.

A tall, lanky boy with hollow cheeks broke through the circle and jutted his face within inches of mine. His faded ink skin hung on his gaunt bones, and his yellow teeth reeked of raw tobacco, a revolting odor.

I stood still as he fingered my flaxen hair.

A muscular boy firmly placed his hand on the boy's shoulder. Saying "Ethan, *respecte*," he gently removed the boy's hand.

"*Merci*," I said.

"Ethan—" He tapped his temple, indicating Ethan wasn't all there. He smiled shyly.

Another boy bounced forward on an imaginary pogo stick.

"I'm Pierre." Pointing to my rescuer, he added, "He's Henri." Leaning forward and assuming an intimate tone, he whispered, "I'm hongry, Madame. Pleez." He brandished an open hand and an irresistible smile.

I shook my head and walked toward the stairs.

A six-foot-three, broad-shouldered man dripping in gold chains and wearing an aloha-style shirt blocked my path. My stomach churned at the cold hate visible on his jet-black face as he stared at me.

Suddenly, he lunged toward the boys. In a staccato, harsh dialect, he verbally assaulted them and physically shooed them away.

Like flies.

His gold teeth sparkled in a sneering laugh as he barked something in Kreyol and strutted off.

A younger fellow in his late teens, wearing a tweed jacket and carrying a long stick, took up the unfinished assault and attempted to hit them.

Whack! The boys skittered about. Most ran away. Pierre and several others tried to hide behind me.

We were all moving in circles when Hans appeared at the top of the stairs, calling, "What's keeping you?"

I raced up the stairs to official introductions and then to the mailbox. Hans bent to retrieve the mail.

"Did you see that man?" I asked.

"You mean the one with gold chains and long shirt?"

"Yes."

"Paramilitary, also known as *attachés* here. They carry guns under those shirts. Stay out of Haitian politics. Let's go, lots to do before we head for the Plateau."

CHAPTER TWO

"The fellow is roasting water."

— *HAITIAN PROVERB*

I didn't see the street boys again for three weeks. I was in the town of Pignon on the Central Plateau in a state of *immersion*, a polite word for being dunked in a culture, living as the natives do with a native family.

The Central Plateau with its rich, intense colors filled me with contentment. Rising early, I walked the few miles to Le Jeune, the twenty-acre missionary compound. I can still feel the morning coolness and see clouds tinged with pink. I always paused on the bridge over the serpentine river and admired the mist lazily rising and shafts of sunlight on water. As the first women descended to wash their clothing, baskets on their heads, they called *bonjour* greetings.

Women on way to wash clothing in river

Child with red hair – second degree malnutrition

Along the way, I might kick dust swirls as I did as a child while contemplating all I needed to learn. Our programs were huge, and being on the Plateau enabled me to see firsthand how they operated. Mother-Child Health, Adult Literacy, Agriculture, and Leadership Development. Each program had a chief coordinator.

On other days, I recalled certain conversations or observations with my Haitian family, whom I loved. While I was to learn Haitian Kreyol from the matron of the family, the practical lessons from immersion came not from my living situation, but from two vastly different street hustlers.

Between them, they taught me nuances of Haitian culture that were not in books or on flash cards or even in a Haitian home. In Pignon, Hugo and Adam were from different sides of the track even without a railroad.

I encountered Hugo first when he leaped from a store front porch and spread his arms in front of me. Streetwise, an in-your-face twenty-five-year old, Hugo clamored for "one dolla, *Blan*," while grabbing my sunglasses and shouting he wanted a *kado, kado*! (gift). Frightened, I jerked backward only for him to dance around me, kicking up yellow dust. It took some demanding and finally, anger to retrieve my sunglasses. I didn't like him.

Adam, on the other hand, must have spotted me in town, for he calculatingly approached me in the park, if the open dirt space with a single tree, a weathered bench and plentiful weeds could be called a park. Carrying a notebook and a pen, luxuries in rural Haiti, he joined me on the bench.

In his early thirties, slim, hair closely cropped, he came to practice his English. I came to be alone.

Since the word *alone* is nonexistent in the Haitian experience, I decided to make the best of it, help him with English and practice my beginning Kreyol.

We had established a language routine when the street hustler appeared. As Hugo sat on the back of the bench with his feet on the seat, I observed his rundown shoes with many holes.

Ignoring Hugo, Adam resumed his lessons while Hugo remained perched on the bench like an uninterested crow. But my Kreyol pronunciation got the better of him. Impatient with my atrocities, his full purple lips exaggerated the vowel sounds. His hand gracefully drew the "o" sound from his rounded lips, and then smoothed the "ahh" sound into the dust. The "eeh" sound roused him from the bench, into my face so that I could clearly see the position of his tongue to his tobacco-stained teeth.

The rancid odor nearly knocked me over.

For the English portion, Hugo could care less. But diligent Adam scrawled English words and complete sentences on his notepad, making sure we clarified verbs and grammatical structure. A teacher's dream.

Hugo interrupted with his first real communication, which he asked through Adam as translator.

"What is your name?"

"Madame Charlotte Wright."

Hugo repeated my name twice, glanced at Adam and scornfully shook his head.

I understood his disbelief. In Haiti, a woman is known by the last name of her husband or a live-in lover called a *plase*. So it is the man's name that provides the identity and social place of the woman.

"I do not have a husband. I am only Madame Charlotte."

Their eyebrows rose. It was incomprehensible that I had no man in my life, no husband, no lover. No one is alone in Haiti.

As we prepared to leave the square, in exaggerated English and smiling all the while, Adam said, "I li-i-ke Ameri-Ken (pause) silver." He flashed his broad smile with gorgeous teeth, continuing, "Do you have (pause, big grin for the *Blan*) Ameri-Kan silver?"

"No, I don't have silver."

His disappointment was only momentary before he asked, "Will you pray for me?"

He waited expectantly. I stared.

"Here? Now?"

"A six-second prayer, maybe seven, not a minute."

I uttered a six-second prayer. "Dear Lord, we thank you for this day. Please bless Adam and Hugo, help them and guide them. In Christ's name. Amen."

Adam was genuinely pleased as though my prayer carried special intercessory powers. He immediately asked that I go with him to his home and see his baby, who was "ill with teething."

When I agreed, the uninvited Hugo accompanied us.

From a narrow dirt road, we turned down a path near a cockfighting arena. Actually, the path was a two-foot gully lined with thick cacti hedges, and it wound past thatched-roof mud huts posted on hard earth. Washed clothing lay evenly spread upon small thorns of cacti.

At the end of the path stood Adam's concrete block house with a tin roof, measuring around fifteen feet square. His home was conveniently situated next to a cornfield belonging to his father-in-law. In addition to helping his father-in-law with corn harvests, he helped his father-in-law and wife sell used American shoes in the marketplace. More than anything, Adam wanted a job in the Pignon hospital.

Written in French and chalked on the green door were the sign of the cross and the words in French, "Adam believes in the return of Jesus Christ and the cross." He explained that this public affirmation prevented evil spirits from entering his home at night and harming his wife and child. He had learned French in school, but as with thousands of Haitians without tuition money, he had been forced to abandon his education.

I stepped over the threshold onto a freshly swept dirt floor. His baby had "headache fever," but they had no money for a doctor.

This was the hungry season, between corn harvests, the time of late afternoon thundershowers, the time of "typhoid-malaria." Since Adam did not know what ailed his son, we talked about reducing fever and providing oral rehydration.

Sweltering in the humidity, I sat on a wooden lawn chair in his 7 x 8 living room as the afternoon rain began to beat upon the tin roof. Raising our voices, we decided that Adam and Hugo could tutor me daily for an hour for ten gourdes each per day.

At that time, this sum translated to seventy-seven cents a day for each one. Since the effects of the American embargo had shrunk the Haitian daily income to about sixty-eight cents a day, a payment of seventy-seven cents was a gift of good fortune. Adam could take his baby to the Catholic Clinic.

Each afternoon our sessions began with the expected polite greetings in Kreyol. Failure to inquire was to be rude. "How are you? How is your family? Have you eaten today?" Most often, Adam and Hugo had not eaten. "Did you eat last night?" Their terse answers conveyed a tacit understanding, as though a single word could portray a living image of how they fared.

As our lessons progressed, both Adam and I translated sentences and took notes.

Accentuating each word, Adam asked about parts of the body, the aches and symptoms of pain. "Do you have a fever?" "Does your stomach hurt?"

Hugo was curious about life in America and what I might buy for him.

I asked about how they lived. I learned they bathed daily in the river and carried water to their homes. In outlying villages, some children or mothers walked three hours or more to obtain water in five-gallon drums.

I learned Hugo had not attended school beyond first grade, and therefore, could not understand French, only Kreyol. His widowed mother owned a small piece of land outside of Pignon where his brothers helped her with a small crop of beans. Without tools, weeds grew freely, and without animals, the soil was dug by hand. When the harvest came, she sold beans in the marketplace, but between harvests, they were hungry.

Like many Haitians, Hugo considered tilling the soil as slave labor, beneath him, a throwback attitude to Haiti's slave history. He preferred other endeavors, but without education, his native intelligence was spent on gambling.

Around the third day, Hugo insisted upon re-directing Adam's planned medical lesson. Sitting forward on his chair, he indicated to Adam he had urgent information.

Displeased with Hugo's interruption, Adam reluctantly translated. "He says, 'Madame Charlotte, if I do not tell you, how can you know?'" Aside he added, "That's a Haitian proverb."

Essentially, Hugo's lessons centered around Haiti's dramas, conning, and being conned, and the critical importance of being both polite and clever. Politeness and cleverness, bedrocks of Haitian values.

Hugo recalled the day he had grabbed my sunglasses.

"When someone wants your sunglasses as a *kado*, (a gift) be polite. Say, 'I'm sorry, but I need these glasses to shield my light eyes from the sun.'"

Adam interjected, "The doctor gave these to me; they are prescription, so I cannot part with them."

Hugo continued. "When children surround you, pressing the *blan* for one dolla', be polite. Say, 'I'm sorry. I regret that you are in need, but I do not have one dolla' today.'"

Pignon Saturday Market

Learning to be clever required learning how to navigate market negotiations, so we scheduled our trio meeting for early Saturday morning, market day. However, Adam came down with chicken pox, leaving Hugo and me to explore market intricacies.

Hugo and I ambled through the primitive marketplace, surveying baskets of vegetables and wooden tables piled with entrails and raw meats and swarming flies. I gagged at both the sight and the stench.

Hugo approached two elderly women who sold tiny kerosene lamps welded from evaporated milk cans with wicks of unprocessed cotton and elaborately painted. I watched as he role-played the bargaining and explained price ranges.

Then came my turn. I was aware of gathering onlookers who leaned forward to hear every word. Would the *Blan* pay the price asked? Would the *marchand* fool the *Blan* to everyone's enjoyment? Who would be the cleverest?

Next, Hugo suggested I choose some vegetables for Adam, and he, the master, would critique my efforts.

As we perused the baskets of vegetables and rice, Hugo said, "Adam is eating dough water, Madame Charlotte. He feeds his wife and child. There is not enough food for him, too."

Silently, I envisioned Adam mixing his meal of flour paste. Always smiling, Adam had never complained of his hunger. Nor had Hugo. I would learn that the phenomenal capacity to endure hardship after hardship without open complaint is a cardinal hallmark of Haitian character.

Hugo insisted upon walking me to Adam's home, even though he had never had the chicken pox. I insisted he remain outside while I delivered the food.

No. With a flick of his hand, he brusquely discounted my objections. He had decided to enter, and that was that. Stubborn. Stubborn to the core, another cardinal hallmark of Haitian character.

After ten days, a turning point occurred in my living situation. With my rapid loss of weight and challenges with boiling drinking water, I was physically unwell.

At the insistence of the American couple who operated Le Jeune Mission, I moved there until Hans would collect me. Although the grounds held a dormitory and cabins, I stayed in the main house guest room.

Mary and I were changing bed sheets when she asked how long I had been divorced.

"Almost seven years."

She studied me. "I'll bet you've had opportunities to remarry."

I snapped a sheet over the bed. "No one seemed right. Someone said I wasn't emotionally available."

Subject closed. She gave a brief smile with a nod.

That evening a torrential thunderstorm pounded on the tin roof. We huddled close to the crackling radio to hear BBC's breaking news about Haiti. The United Nations announced that in an effort to force the military dictatorship to resign and allow Aristide to return as President, they had voted to place an oil and arms embargo on the nation of Haiti, effective immediately.

Mary covered her eyes and muttered something incoherent. Tom placed his fists on his thighs, stood and walked to the window where rain lashed the panes.

"What's this mean?" I asked.

Mary's voice smarted with agitation. "It means that thousands are going to die of starvation, mostly children and old people, and--"

Tom calmly interrupted. "Charlotte, the U.N. embargo on oil changes everything. If you're going to keep your programs operating, you'll have to conserve fuel for operations. That means restricting gas for vehicles and diesel fuel for office generators."

I sank into the back of the sofa. "How? I just got here."

A thunderclap rolled through the room, drowning his voice.

"What?" I shouted.

"Determine the hours at the office that the generator can run. The electricity shortage in Port-au-Prince will worsen. You need to be ready. Limit the trips of the trucks. Make those decisions as soon as possible. In fact, tonight I'll shut down the generator at eight."

My head reeled. "What will happen here?"

Bitter sadness spilled from Mary. "The international aid programs will close. Internationals will leave. They'll go home to warm meals and soft beds. Even rich Haitians will leave. You'll see. Just the poor will suffer."

I recalled the four Haitian employees on the Plateau who, only two weeks earlier, had beseeched Hans for a food program for their children. I pictured the street boys at Lynx Air office who begged and depended upon the handouts from internationals. Mostly though, I thought about my fourteen-year-old daughter, Shelley, who soon would be arriving for school.

"Come on, Char, let's have some brownies and coffee." Mary pulled me from the sofa.

"No coffee for me," I said as Mary handed me the kerosene lamp for the dining table.

I sat down and put my head in my hands. "I don't know if I

can do this job. Maybe I should quit. I'm a physical wreck. I'm lonely, and I'm worried about Shelley."

"I thought Shelley wanted to come. Didn't she say she was looking forward to the great adventure?" She cocked her head to one side, appraising me.

I smiled at the pixie image of my little one. "She does, but she doesn't know what it's like. And now this, this oil embargo thing--"

"Sounds like you're the one having second thoughts."

I nodded.

"You're exhausted. You need a good night's sleep."

A comfortable silence rested upon us as she cut the brownies.

"I'm not saying it's easy, Charlotte. We've spent twenty years here, and Tom has worked hard to train Haitians, how to care for crops and equipment. But you know what? When we leave, the land will revert to weeds, and the equipment will rust. Nothing we've done here will last. Haiti is Haiti."

"Then what's it all about?"

"Doing the best you can while you're here. Helping people at a basic level, giving birth, immunizations, learning to read. Doing what God wants you to do, regardless of the outcome."

"How will I know what to do?"

"You'll know. It's what God puts on your heart to do. Your organization selected you because they saw something in you. They saw enough to send a woman into this domineering male culture. That speaks for itself. They believe in you, Charlotte. Believe in yourself. Believe in God."

As I rose, she said, "Think about why you *really* came to Haiti."

CHAPTER THREE

"How you beat the drum is how we dance."

— HAITIAN PROVERB

Immersed, I returned to Port-au-Prince, speaking minimal Kreyol and naturally, encountered the begging, pushy street boys. No thank you, not for me. They represented that pool of general begging, that dangerous arena of being "on-call" for money to solve their problems. I would not go there.

Hans had left for Canada, and my first order of business was to implement Tom's suggestions. I studied reports and trips, made calculations, and thereby, placed restrictions on fuel and oil.

At my rented home on a hillside in Petionville, I hung mosquito nets, installed an inverter, purchased multiple kerosene lamps and kept Arthur, the housekeeper who had worked for Hans.

Our house on a hill overlooking city

The house was located on an alley-sized road that came to a dead-end, making it difficult to find. With the garage below, the living quarters were on the second floor. Across the tiny street was a yawning ravine hidden behind a wall of blooming pink oleanders, a lovely sight from the bank of louvered windows in the living room, windows that welcomed sea breezes.

A safe gate divided the large, open living-kitchen area

from the hall to the bedrooms, but we always left the gate open. The sizeable balcony overlooked the city and was accessible from both the living area and the master bedroom. It was perfect. A refuge. Equilibrium.

I ensured equilibrium through routine: attend language lessons at Presse Evangelique, go to the office for the day, go home. Change, drive to the Hotel Villa Creole for the day's gossip with Americans who ran manufacturing firms, and then usually, enjoy a French dinner alone at one of four restaurants. Home. Shower. Read. Pray. Sleep. An orderly life.

Incorporating Hugo's politeness lessons, I still never gave to beggars, even to the handful of street boys who sniffed out my routine. They decided their daily visits should become part of my equilibrium.

So, there they sat, as they did every morning when I left Presse Evangelique. Playing with twigs, they sat idly on the curb by my red Trooper SUV, which they called "Madame's machine."

The moment the boys saw me, they leaped and scurried, instantly launching their pitches.

"Madame, Madame. *Mwen ginyin yon pwoblem.*"(I've got a problem.) Always, each boy whispered his name. "I'm Emil. Remember me." Or Philippe, or Jacques, or whoever. Always, the problem could be remedied with money. My money.

I never gave.

As I crossed the street, four more came running.

"Madame, Madame," called a little one still twenty-five yards away and racing full speed, "a little something for guarding your machine."

"Guarding? I saw you running down the street. What were you guarding? My machine's not down there."

The boys laughed, and one jocularly rubbed the small one's head.

The little boy's angular clavicle protruded above his oversized t-shirt splotched with food stains and dirt. His bony legs extended beneath a pair of brown shorts, reminding me of a child's drawing of a stickman wearing baggy drawers.

"I'm Jean, Madame." He grinned impishly.

"How old are you?"

"Probably eight, maybe seven," answered a boy at my elbow.

I turned. The boy beamed a recognizable smile with mischievous eyes.

"Bo'jour, Madame, I'm Pierre. Remember me?"

I smiled, remembering our first encounter at Lynx Air office.

"Madame," he whispered, "Madame, *m'ginyin yon pwoblem.*" He pulled a crumpled paper from his pocket and thrust it toward me.

Taking it, I struggled to decipher the medical prescription written in French. I looked back at Pierre.

He tugged at the over-stretched neck of his faded red t-shirt and then, waiting, poked his finger through a hole forming at his belly button. From living barefoot, his feet had widened, and his toes spread apart naturally. Dried mud cupped his soles like a pair of worn slippers.

"What is this?"

"Madame. My sister is sick and needs medicine, but we have no money."

He looked aside. In misery. The boys watched quietly.

I studied the French again, wondering what to do. Often the poor could see a doctor, but weren't able to fill prescriptions. The medicine cost more than a doctor's visit, or after a visit, they had no remaining money to purchase the medicine.

I licked my lips and thought, *Maybe I should give*. Then I saw the date.

"Nice try, Pierre, this prescription is three months old."

I chuckled and handed it back to him.

He slapped me on the arm and laughed. "You read French, Madame!"

The boys laughed, and a few clapped as though they had seen a good play. Pierre patted me again in a congratulatory manner.

Although I felt the grime on his fingers, I liked the human touch. A pang shot through me. I missed Shelley. She would have enjoyed Pierre's con.

In true Haitian form, Pierre's companion from the curb performed an exaggerated re-enactment of the attempted con. He handed me the prescription again. I studied the prescription, then pointed to the date and handed it back to him. The boys pushed each other, and everyone laughed again.

Still chortling, the companion said, "Madame, Pierre doesn't have a sister."

Feigning shock, I said, "No-o."

"This is Adrien, Madame." Pierre threw his scrawny arm around Adrien's neck. "My best friend."

Both boys were thirteen or fourteen years old. Lithe and handsome, Adrien's light brown eyes bespoke a tender heart. He possessed a natural grace, like a gazelle.

Mischief and spontaneity were Pierre's trademarks. When he flashed his broad smile, he was guileless. I marveled how a street boy could retain such innocence.

"Pleez, Madame, some money for food. I'm hongry," he said, rubbing his stomach for emphasis and poking his finger through the shirt hole again. "A little something."

I considered my resolve about giving, but Hans' admonition echoed. *Give, and you'll be on the hook forever.* Selfishly, I simply didn't want to become involved, particularly on a daily basis and particularly with a group of street kids.

"I'm sorry for your need, but not today."

Pierre reached for the car keys in my hand.

I pulled them away. "No," I said, unlocking the car door and climbing in.

"Can we ride in the machine?" Pierre begged.

"No, I'm going to work."

"Drive us to Lynx Air. We want to ride in the machine," whined one of the twins who were about ten years old.

"No-o," I said, starting the engine.

In the rear-view mirror, I watched them slowly disperse as I did every day after my Kreyol lessons. Turning the corner, I headed down a one-way avenue, shifting the gear.

Every day we linger and joke, and every day, I leave with a warm feeling.

Ironically, when I broke my private pledge not to give, it wasn't for Pierre or Adrien. It was for Josef and Louie, whom I had occasionally seen, but they were not part of the usual welcoming committee.

These two had the smarts to find me on the school grounds and not outside on the streets. They stopped me on the entrance stairs.

The tall boy, around fifteen, was black as coal and barefooted. Pointing to his post-pubescent bony feet, he announced in a clipped bass voice, "I need shoes for school."

I recognized his blue gingham shirt as one belonging to a school uniform. Yet school had not yet begun, and the shirt was strikingly too small.

He pursed his lips for a stern effect. "Without shoes, I cannot go to school."

I did the unthinkable. I turned to the short, much younger boy and asked, "Is this true? Does he go to school?"

Of course! But wait! There's more! Not only Josef goes to school, but he, himself, Louie, also attends school! Jumping up and down, grinning, he pointed to his fast-moving bare feet. "I need shoes, too!"

Something touched me about the pair, the older one with the gruff manner and protective air and the younger one with bouncing enthusiasm. Maybe I just really wanted them to be in school.

"How much are shoes?"

"Three dollars. Haitian, not American," the younger boy rapidly responded.

"No, four," countered the older one.

Smothering their grins, they exchanged glances.

"Five," they quickly agreed, and their hands shot out in unison and anticipation.

"Five dollars?" I asked with mock disbelief.

"Haitian, not American!" Louie exclaimed.

"For A-mer-i-kan tennis shoes at the Petionville market," said the older boy, breaking his stern expression.

"*Kal-i-te!*" underscored the little one who was all teeth.

Faking a stern expression of my own and opening my purse, I said, "I'll give you each four dollars. But I expect to see your shoes tomorrow. If you don't buy shoes with this money, I'll remember you, and I'll never give you anything again."

Not that I had ever given; nor did I intend to.

The older boy nodded in fierce agreement while biting his lips to smother open laughter. The younger one counted each dollar as I placed it in his hand.

As I watched them race out the gate, I felt smug, convinced my harsh admonition worked. *They're off to spend their treasure elsewhere, and they won't return to me.*

How totally naïve.

The Haitian grapevine already was telegraphing the message, "The *blan* madame who studies at 8:00 a.m. at Presse Evangelique gave money for tennis shoes. *Kal-i-te!*"

On the steps of Presse Evangelique the following morning, the older one stood like a drill sergeant and proudly pointed down to his used white tennis shoes. The little one danced to unheard rhythms, shaking his agile body as he twisted his foot in the air, displaying his black tennis shoes.

Several boys lounging against a wall sauntered into the yard and openly admired Louie's flair and success in obtaining the best bargain. His black shoes were not only *kal-i-te*; they were fashionable!

Naturally, they all needed shoes for school. Even a well-dressed passerby entered the yard, removed a shoe and, pointing to a tiny hole in the sole, demanded he also be given money for shoes.

I slapped my head and entered the building.

After that, occasionally when Pierre, Adrien or Henri, my muscular rescuer from Mad Ethan on day one at Lynx Air, were alone, I gave them "a little something," but not often. In fact, the four or five boys waiting daily by my SUV had even stopped asking for money. Once I overheard one tell a newcomer who began his plea, "She never gives."

Nevertheless, they still came and settled for conversation.

"Oh Madame, your Kreyol is better."

"Where are you going? Can we ride in the machine?"

"What is the Central Plateau like?"

"Do you have children?"

"Three," I answered. "Two boys and a girl."

They wanted to know where they were. When they learned my daughter was fourteen and would be arriving in early August, their excitement knew no bounds.

Pierre immediately bounced on his imaginary pogo stick. "Fourteen? I'm fourteen. Madame's daughter is my age!"

A laughing Adrien asked, "What's her name?"

"Shelley."

Simultaneously, they practiced saying Shelley's name, while pushing and shoving one another, correcting each other's efforts.

"Shel-LEE, SHEL-lee. Mademoiselle SHEL-LEE."

They were filled with curiosity. "Can she speak Kreyol? Can she read? Can Mademoiselle Shel-lee write? Is she pretty?"

I came to look forward to our jovial banter and now handed my keys to Pierre or Adrien who unlocked the SUV.

But one morning as I was leaving, Pierre and the twins appeared with a weeping Adrien whose head had been shaved. In uncontrollable sobbing, Adrien moaned, "I'm innocent. I'm innocent."

Pierre, the twins and several others held his arms in comfort, and all were mumbling, "a cappie."

"Pleez, Madame Charlotte. Give money to Adrien for a cappie." Pierre made the motion of putting on a baseball cap.

I looked at Adrien's bald head and his tortured eyes.

"He's not a thief," muttered a twin.

At the word *thief*, all shook their heads and concurred that Adrien was not a thief.

Pierre took a breath and instructed me like a patient teacher. "Madame Charlotte, in the market, a *marchand* accused Adrien of stealing, and an *attaché* shaved his head." He held up his hands as if to say the story was finished.

"Why?"

"Because that's the punishment. It's shame."

At that comment, Adrien wailed and rubbed his head.

"I'm innocent, Madame. I didn't steal anything."

I studied his mocha face of finely chiseled features and

pleading eyes. I believed him. Adrien was a street boy in the wrong place at the wrong time. He did not deserve the visual stigma allocated to criminals.

Without a word, I opened my purse. Everyone quieted in that thought-filled moment. I gave the money to Adrien and only nodded to his sincere expressions of gratitude.

"Merci, Madame Charlotte. *Merci, merci."*

They started down the street, but Adrien turned, ran back and thanked me again. Even as he left, he looked back, shouting, *"Merci!"*

As I crossed the street, I realized a new forging had occurred between that handful of street boys and me.

There was a mutual understanding in our silence, a message in our eyes that said to me, "These children are in great need," and said to them, "Here is a *Blan* who understands we have problems."

CHAPTER FOUR

"You are the moth. I am the lamp."

— *HAITIAN PROVERB*

Regardless of the street hustle or the con, the hunger of the *timoun nan lari-yo*, children of the street, was real. Their hunger was real before the American and U.N. embargos, but generous internationals and optimism had kept them reasonably fed. After the announcement of the embargo, the internationals re-assessed their commitments to Haiti and gradually began to close. The mood further dimmed with inflated food prices and insecurity. Begging required more struggle.

I found myself giving more frequently to the boys who appeared every morning: Pierre, Adrien, Henri, the twins and a newcomer, Lucas.

Lucas wore intensity well. Large, dark eyes, slight frame with glossy black skin, beautiful teeth, and full lips. He was the serious one. Also around fourteen, the boys told me Lucas often stayed with prostitutes. One morning he showed up riding a bicycle. We all stared as he glided by.

Henri chuckled. Placing one hand into the palm of the other, he flicked his hands together Haitian style. "By this afternoon, no bicycle."

I began taking "to go" bags of food from the restaurants at night because I knew several would be "guarding my machine." We engaged in silly jesting and laughter, and taking the food and my keys, they opened the door of my machine. Always, I rolled down the window for farewells. A quick hand would push down the lock, and a voice admonished me to pay attention.

It is not surprising that their numbers grew from four to seven, then ten, still only the beginning. The smell of money was the aroma of food. After the morning class, I began entering the machine and locking the door before I rolled down the window to distribute money for a day's ration.

From our chatter, I learned a three-gourde meal would fill them for most of the day while a five-gourde meal would fill them for the whole day. When a larger number appeared, I gave for a three-gourde meal; otherwise, I provided a five-gourde meal.

Marchand *cooking stew*

Most boys usually purchased their meals from the *marchands* selling stew from iron cauldrons cooking over charcoal fires. Others purchased rice and beans for their mothers or friends to cook over small charcoal grills.

Their cracked, dirty hands stretched to clasp their gourdes as they pushed and shoved to reach the window. "Madame Charlotte, my name is so-and-so" each shouted, etching his identity into my memory, only to be pushed aside as another skinny arm reached upward.

I came to dread those moments of distribution. It was hard enough to bear their hunger, but the desperate chaos bore witness to their raw struggle for survival.

When the daily number reached ten to twelve, I said, "I'm sorry for your need. But I have only so much money. When that money is gone, I can't give any more. Do you understand?"

They nodded, for most certainly they understood scarcity. Still, that unhappy fact increased their anxiety, and the pushing and shoving worsened. After the distribution, each boy raced away to protect his treasure. The unsuccessful ones trailed away.

One morning when Pierre had failed to reach the window, he bent over and holding his stomach, staggered to the wall and cried. I saw him in the rearview mirror.

"Pierre, Pierre," I whispered to the mirror, "you are not made for the streets."

I shifted to reverse and called him.

As he came to the SUV, he wiped his tears, smearing the dirt on his face. I observed again the cracks and wrinkles on his hands and fingers like that of someone decades older.

"*Merci*, Madame Charlotte," he said, a grin on his baby face. "*Merci*," he shouted and waved as he dashed away.

I put my head on the steering wheel.

Naturally, the entreaties for money extended to desires other than food. They wanted *rad*, nice clothing. Haitians pride themselves on their appearance, and the street boys were no different. They pointed out their t-shirts with holes or tattered pants.

I avoided that rabbit hole.

Adrien and Pierre sometimes called me "Mama." Crossing my arms, I calmly said, "I'm not your Mama."

They laughed.

"You're *grunmoun*," said Pierre. An old person, an incredibly old person.

I scowled. Pierre laughed again.

Adrien slapped his thigh. "No, no, Madame Charlotte, *grunmoun* is an old, wise person. Very wise."

His eyes twinkled, and genuine warmth emanated. I enjoyed the special rapport he and Pierre shared, sheer entertainment for each other. For me, too.

And the boys wanted to read. And write.

Adrien had loved school, but had to quit in second or third grade. Henri had completed third grade. Always the same story: schools charge tuition. No money.

"Madame Charlotte, I want to read," whispered Pierre.

Their pleas to read held a different tenor than the usual begging. It was a still-water, quiet yearning they could barely express, as though to mention it aloud might frighten hope.

I saw them every morning at Presse Evangelique school and also at Lynx Air in late afternoon.

Unfortunately, I also saw the usual paramilitary *attaché* with his expression of hate, wearing an aloha shirt that covered his probable nine-millimeter gun. Victor and his stick were nearby as well.

Around eighteen, Victor was the young man who usually brandished his long stick and mercilessly bullied the boys. Wearing a tweed jacket in the tropical heat, he raised his stick and whacked someone while others scattered.

As for me, the boys now bantered more than begged. Humor ruled the day. The swarm of flies upon the fruit stopped. In fact, when several would beg from me, someone would say, "Madame Charlotte gave to you this morning."

Yet one request caused a ruckus among all.

Lucas, now *sans* bicycle, said, "Madame Charlotte, please buy us a soccer ball."

Excitement generated like lightning after a thunderclap.

"Where would you play?"

"In the big park."

"Yes, yes, in the big park," came the echoes of excitement.

"Where would you keep the ball?"

Only a brief uncertainty. Eyes searched each other.

Someone blurted, "Henri. Henri lives with his mother. He can keep the ball."

I smiled to myself, recalling years of enjoyment I had when my children had played. "Where do we buy a ball?"

Victory roared with that question! Everyone wanted to

give directions to a small shop that sold school supplies and soccer balls.

Across the street from Lynx Air office sat the usual group of *marchands,* their skirts loosely gathered around their knees, hair wrapped in colorful scarves. Their baskets displayed eggplants, sweet potatoes, pumpkins, lettuce, tomatoes and onions. I saw them laughing as the swarm re-emerged, encircling me.

Undoubtedly, the Haitian grapevine was telegraphing the message, "Madame Charlotte is buying a soccer ball for the *timoun nan lari-yo.*"

At home, my routine included my inherited housekeeper in his thirties. Due to the oil embargo, electricity was erratic, and our evening light usually came from kerosene lamps.

While I worked by lamp, Arthur wore my Walkman and listened to tapes of popular American music. He was so still that I looked over to check him and observed his lanky body slumped in a chair, head back and his chocolate complexion dotted with sweat.

Regardless of how late I worked, Arthur sat by the desk with me until I retired. He then locked up and went to his room, which was a tiny shed behind the house. I was shocked when I saw it. A tiny room, perhaps 8 x 8, with a small louvered window, and in the heat, it must have been stifling. Fortunately, he spent his days and early evenings in the house.

I could gauge Arthur's frame of mind by the degree of swishing. If he were happy, he swished down the stairs to the garage, his arms happily swinging. If unhappy, he slowly loped. In the days prior to Shelley's arrival, his swishing almost made noise.

CHAPTER FIVE

"Little by little, the bird builds its nest."

— HAITIAN PROVERB

The Airport boys veered and thundered toward us as we entered the parking lot. Shelley froze. I stepped in front of her and held up my hand to stop them.

I pointed to two boys. "You and you. Here. Take these."

The two seized the bags and fell behind us in orderly fashion. When others surrounded us and clamored, I shook my head.

"*Mwen regretsa, no jodia.*" (I'm sorry, not today.)

Taking Shelley's elbow, I pulled her close to me and ushered her to the SUV.

After the boys had placed the bags in my machine, I opened my purse and said, "*Merci*. A little something."

The other boys watched my payment in silence. No fuss.

"That wasn't as bad as you said." She stretched her legs in the front seat.

I smiled to myself.

A typical Haitian **tap**-tap *(taxi)*

As we drove through congestion to Petionville, I watched Shelley's face. Nothing seemed to amaze or repel her.

Sitting by me was a bright-eyed young girl, full of curiosity.

We stopped behind a Haitian taxi called *tap-tap*, an elaborately decorated, elongated truck with an open rear. The inner benches overflowed with people to the extent that the *tap-tap* lisped. A hand-painted Madonna adorned the sides of the rear entry. Enlarged, puckered red lips perched above the entry provided a welcome.

We laughed out loud.

At home, Arthur waited at the garage door, happy to welcome her and swishing with her bags.

Shelley and her dog, Bandit

Except for the tiger-swirled tile floor, Shelley approved the house and location. Her sizeable bedroom already held a mosquito net, and she had her own bath. Since the house had a water catchment, we at least would have cold water.

When we headed for the half-day registration at School the next morning, we were nervous.

"New beginnings," I said, parking in front.

Shelley just sat there.

"Mom, what's with the rolled barbed wire on top of the fence?" Then she studied the guard gate entry. "And guards with machine guns?"

My heart sank. How could I be so stupid? I had forewarned her about the Saturday night *Vodou* ceremonies and drums in the ravine, but I had forgotten the M-16's!

I felt like a failure. Again. I tried to explain that guards with guns are everywhere in Haiti, at stores, at banks. In such a short time, I had become so accustomed to seeing them, I didn't think to prepare her.

"Why does a school need guards with machine guns? I mean, I can understand the rolled barbed wire thing, maybe, like computers and all. But machine guns?"

My tongue stumbled over the words. "Influential Haitian families and international diplomats send their kids here. They want to know they're protected."

"From what?"

"Political upheaval, I guess. Kidnappings. Whatever."

Shelley was quiet for a moment, then said with heated disgust, "You *never* think about the bad stuff, Mom. You only see the good. You are such a dreamer!"

I closed my eyes, feeling my breath collapse within me, as it always did in the heat of her anger. Particularly when she was right.

"Take your foot off the dashboard."

She removed her foot.

"You look nice in the uniform. I like the yellow polo."

She looked down at her polo shirt with the School insignia.

Squeezing her arm, I said, "You'll like the Principal. I think you'll like the school."

"You sure she agreed to promote me?"

I nodded. "Yes, we had a long conversation. You will be in the ninth grade." I glanced at my watch. "Time to go in."

Inside, I signed Shelley in and turned her over to the Principal. "See you at noon."

At noon, her mood was more relaxed. Enumerating her

courses on her fingers, she cited English, Math, Social Studies, and P.E.

"There's a new teacher from Canada for Science; she seems good. I have to take French. Did you know that?"

"French is the national language. Did you sign-up for the tennis team?"

"That's the best part. We play in Puerto Rico and the Dominican Republic. How 'bout that? I get to go to other countries."

This is good, I thought. The first enthusiasm I had heard about school in a long time.

I started the SUV and pulled out of the parking lot. "Meet any new friends?"

"Maybe. Marilyn. She's American, showed me around. Her dad's with the government, CIA probably. Marilyn says they live on the mountain, and he has a lot of radio equipment in a private room."

As we pulled into the Lynx Air parking lot, a swarm of boys headed for us.

Shelley vigorously slapped on the door lock several times, even though it was already locked.

"It's okay. They're curious about you. Do what I told you.

Keep walking. If they ask for money, say 'No, I'm sorry.' Wait until I come around to your side before you open the door."

I had navigated the throng to the front of the machine when Shelley ventured to open her door and get out. She entered the surrounding boys like a reluctant swimmer wading into cold water.

I saw Ethan from a distance, and though I pushed and shoved, I could not get past the adjacent parked car.

Ethan, the gangly, mentally challenged boy reached out, pulled a strand of Shelley's hair, running his fingers over it.

Shelley froze. "Mama? MAMA!"

I scrambled to push through, shouting, "Ethan!"

Henri reached her first and walloped Ethan's head. Ethan instantly released her hair.

"Respecte!" he shouted, pushing Ethan away. Then he pushed other boys back. And when the path was cleared, Henri bowed. "Mademoiselle Shel-lee," he said, flourishing his arm in gallantry to the open path.

Pierre was immediately there. "Mademoiselle Shel-lee, "you go to school?" He started to finger the insignia on the sleeve.

Henri slapped his arm, and Pierre giggled.

Shelley said nothing. She kept a fixed stare ahead where a small group of boys backed up as she walked.

"Shelley, this is Pierre," I said, looping my arm through hers.

Pierre was all teeth. "In English he asked, "Can you read?"

Bewildered, she looked to me.

"He wants to know if you know how to read. Answer him."

"Yes."

Pierre beamed. Turning to others he proclaimed, "Mademoiselle Shel-lee can read! Madame Charlotte, I want to read."

That request launched the chorus.

"Oui."

"I want to read."

"I went to school once."

"Do you read?"

"No."

We passed the ever-present *attaché* because his job was to watch and eavesdrop on internationals. Victor with his stick was also there. However, Victor kept the stick to himself, most likely because he focused on the new arrival.

Messieur Hate laughed aloud in his deep baritone, gold teeth glistening. "The *timoun nan lari-yo* want to read." He chuckled again at the absurdity.

We ignored him.

That evening we attended a welcoming event, a potluck dinner, hosted by the missionaries of my organization. The young Canadian who worked for me in the economic development arm and his wife were also there. For our dish, Shelley and I compiled a refreshing salad of smoked eggplant, mirliton and tomatoes dressed with olive oil and fresh lemon juice.

Arranged neatly, the tables seated about twelve. Although I sensed the chill in the air, I hoped Shelley did not. However, any hope of her escaping the veiled hostility ended with a lengthy blessing before dinner.

Given by a missionary friendly to me, he began with a usual prayer structure. Gratitude, blessings for our bounty, requests for grace and guidance, but with a surprise ending. He genuinely appealed that God open their hearts to forego judgments and receive people who might be different. He added one or two other sentences that clearly had my name on it. Head down, I glanced at Shelley who was squinting at me.

When we were in the car, she asked, "Is this the first time you've been invited?"

"Yeah."

"They don't like you very much."

"No. They didn't like the salad either."

"Why? Because I don't attend the Christian School?"

"In part. Maybe they took it as an insult. And I attend a different church service."

Shelley did not attend the Christian School for several reasons. An independent thinker and non-conformist, Shelley would have been a misfit, attending a school where conformity was the rule and where she would be without friends. In short, she would have been miserable, and the principal ultimately would have expelled her. The tipping point was that the private school near our home had a tennis team, and she was a phenomenal player. The prospect of playing on a tennis team excited her.

"It's more than that," I added. "My regional supervisor is close to the missionary arm here. I expect they adopted his opposition toward me."

"What do you mean?"

"I'm divorced. I'm well-educated. And the third strike: I wasn't his choice. That was the very first thing he said to me when I met him. 'You are not my choice, but I wasn't consulted.'"

"What do you do for friends?"

"I have the street boys." I grinned. "I go to the Hotel Villa Creole on work nights and meet with acquaintances I call my Round Table. You'll meet them."

She was appalled to learn that the Round Table consisted of three, sometimes four, American managers of American manufacturing firms specializing in sewing, and one or two American government employees with U.S. Aid.

"Mom, that's horrible, like slave labor."

"No, they're really not. They provide decent working hours and conditions and pay a decent wage. Sure, it's Haitian, but it's decent. Sorry I can't say that about other countries here. Plus, they know Haiti. They tell me things I need to know."

"Like what?"

"Like when to stay home and what to do in certain

situations. Marcia works for U.S. Aid and keeps us informed of what our government is doing."

Bandit interrupts my work for cuddles

Shelley settled in, with a higher energy level than I had seen in a long time. For that alone, I was happy. Marilyn, the American student, became her friend along with several others, but her best friends were Alex and Mateo.

American and part-Haitian, Alex was a natural intellectual, and they began doing homework together. Colombian, Mateo played the Spanish guitar, and Mateo's father often took them to the country club after school to play tennis.

At the Hotel Villa Creole, regulars were treated like family with full access to amenities. Shelley met her friends there, played tennis or swam while I stayed current on Haitian news with my American acquaintances.

We were laughing about how we now cited the number of hours a day we had electricity rather than the number of hours without it when my favorite waiter, limped to the table.

Attempting to repress his laughter, he said, "Madame Charlotte, Mademoiselle Shelley ordered a Pina Colada. I said I would ask you."

He snickered.

Across the room, at a table with her friends, Shelley waited. Sitting straight, she grinned like a Cheshire cat.

"A virgin Pina Colada."

At night, we frequently worked by kerosene lamp. Shelley completed homework. I focused on operations, writing an application for humanitarian fuel, and wrote a new micro-enterprise program proposal for women.

One evening she said, "There's a girl at school who's hassling me, a big Haitian girl."

"How?"

"Whenever she's near me, she bumps into me or hits me.

She claims it's an accident, but it happens a lot. Today she bumped me, and I stumbled and spilled my drink."

For a moment, Shelley's mask of I-can-handle-anything dropped. "I haven't done anything to her." Her voice choked, and her eyes watered in hurt. "She doesn't even know me."

"Sounds like a bully. Maybe you can introduce yourself again, say something like you don't know what you've done to offend her, but you'd like to be friends."

Silence.

"Just be nice. Keep being nice, and she'll change."

"That's dreaming, Mom."

"It's still good advice."

We were packing boxes for the long drive to Pignon on the Central Plateau when I asked, "How's your situation with the Haitian girl?"

Shelley opened the refrigerator door for peanut butter. "It's okay."

"What'd you do?" I waited expectantly to hear if my high-minded advice had worked.

She mumbled and walked to the kitchen counter.

"What? I didn't hear you."

Shelley whirled, her feet planted apart and shouted, "She pushed me into the locker at P.E., so I slapped her hard and said, 'If you ever bother me again, I'll beat the s—t out of you!" She tossed a loaf of bread into the box. "She hasn't bothered me since."

CHAPTER SIX

"Never put the cat in charge of the lard."

— HAITIAN PROVERB

Six hours for 110 miles. In months to come, the time would be eight hours, and finally, the road would close.

We sailed through the military checkpoint at Mirebelais. The soldier with a cigarette hanging from his lips waved us through. Then came more mountains after mountains in rich palettes of greens and browns.

"Making charcoal," I said, pointing to the numerous plumes of lazy smoke.

I swerved around a fresh branch planted in the narrow road, the first of many on our journey.

"Another broken down car ahead," I said, pointing to the branch.

The tortuous, narrow road switched back and forth as we climbed. In sections of deteriorated asphalt with deep potholes, the SUV rocked over smaller boulders and skirted larger ones. Often the road was only bedrock or sand.

I rolled down the window as we proceeded into another series of hairpins. Perched on a hand-woven straw saddle, a withered woman spanked her emaciated burro into a momentary gallop and passed us. I listened to the sound of her clacking tongue as she switched its dusty hide.

When we passed young girls hauling five-gallon plastic buckets of water, Shelley was surprised. "They're younger than me."

I explained that in the back villages, children and their mothers walk for hours to get water.

"What about school?"

"Girls seldom go to school in the countryside. They stay home, take care of babies and maybe help their mothers sell things in the marketplace."

A kamyonet *transports barrels for black market oil, live chickens and passengers*

Shelley bit her bottom lip. I could see the contrast with her own life soaking in.

Yet the starkest contrast occurred in the high, arid mountain range called the Artibonite. Hungry children by the side of the road extended their scrawny, little hands for money.

"See the red hair?"

She nodded.

"That's a sign of kwashiorkor, severe protein deficiency. That's second-degree malnutrition. The protruding bellies —-see those?"

She nodded.

"That's third-degree malnutrition."

We stopped long enough to give "a little something."

At a rest stop near the lake, we carried our toilet paper and hiked into the bushes, past the rotund, thatched cockfighting arena.

"Like camping," she said. "Is this biodegradable?"

Occasionally, we forded a stream. As we descended among the rocks to the riverbank, a quiet coolness enveloped us. Time ceased. Immense, gray kapok trees with gnarled roots lined the banks and canopied topless women washed clothing on the rocks. Nude children splashed, and their laughter echoed across the water.

As we climbed again, Shelley spotted a circular thatched hut resting in the center of a circle. Surrounding the hut were poles of flags.

"What are the flags?"

"That's the hut of a *hougan*, a *Vodou* witch doctor. Each flag represents the primary *Vodou* god the *hougan* serves, so the peasants know which *hougan* to go to for a particular cause."

"Seven flags," she said.

"Busy man."

The mountains gradually leveled out as we approached the next military checkpoint of Hinche.

I kept what I knew about the Hinche checkpoint to myself. During the military *coup d'état*, Hinche was particularly violent. Now, the military did not appreciate international patter about returning the exiled elected President Aristide to power.

Recently, they had pulled a Haitian non-profit worker from his car and beat him mercilessly, claiming he was an Aristide supporter. However, I held to Hans' view that said Hinche guards left Americans alone and generally did not bother with missionaries. Even though I wasn't technically a missionary, at least I was connected and carried a business card.

Several khaki-uniformed guards stood aimlessly by the white frame building. Blurred images of "Papa Doc"'s" infamous *Tonton Macoute* surfaced in my mind, images of goose-stepping men in brown uniforms and sunglasses with brass stars. Even though the *Macoute* organization had been outlawed, the prospect that the men were still around was scary stuff.

I stopped the SUV, and Shelley opened the glove compartment for the papers. Sitting in the rear, Arthur removed his headphones and sat straight. Arthur knew about Hinche.

A tall, burly lieutenant swaggered toward us. His air of intimidation matched his size, particularly when he claimed the driver's window with his elbows and leaned in to inspect the rear. After I answered his questions and produced the documents, he waved us through.

When we crossed the bridge at Hinche, we arrived on the Central Plateau where the earth vacillated between red ochre and fertile brown, and the cooler air refreshed us. Abundant palm and banana trees graced mud huts with thatched roofs.

Soon, higher grasses and more numerous palm trees bordered a now single lane road of loose dirt and clay. Dried tire ruts sank as deep as ten inches.

"Le Jeune Mission," I said, pulling into the compound.

The following morning, we headed for the farmers' cooperative where a judicial hearing would be held. I borrowed Tom's truck with reliable four-wheel drive since the rains might begin before we returned.

On the road to Pignon, Haitians on their way to Saturday market flagged us down. Since in Haiti, it is polite to stop and give rides, the truck rear was full by the time we rolled into Pignon.

At the cooperative, donkeys were tied to cacti hedges. Wearing their Sunday best, most peasants arrived on foot. They mingled together on the large field before settling on benches erected for the hearing.

"Looks like a painting," said Shelley.

Yes. Vivid red, yellow, and blue headscarves and skirts. Rich earth-black skin against bleached, starched white shirts. Hand-woven straw hats.

The arbitrator from Cap-Haitien perspired in a suit and tie as he waited before a small, primitive wood table. I debated whether to approach him or retire to a corner of the field.

The Farmers' Cooperative gathers

My Hotel Villa Round Table said my organization didn't stand a chance. It did not matter that we were the sponsors, not the owners of the cooperative. My organization was international, and Haitians saw international organizations as geese with golden eggs. "You'll be lucky not to lose thousands."

The case centered on a former manager of the farmers' cooperative who had been sent to Port-au-Prince to purchase seed. However, he purchased three hundred watering cans instead. No seed. The feisty Chairman of the

Board, belching fury, fired him. In retaliation, the manager broke into the office and took the accounting books, which remained in his possession.

The fired manager then opened his own agricultural store across the street from the co-op, and *su-preeze*, as Haitians say, it sold seeds, even tools. Now he was suing the cooperative, therefore, my organization since we sponsored them, for compensation and damages.

The perspiring judge looked solemnly at the gathering crowd. I introduced myself.

"I never expected so many people, maybe fifty at the most. There must be two hundred here." He looked around, possibly searching for a quick exit route.

"They're interested in the outcome of the case," I casually said. "After all, it is their cooperative."

He pulled a fanciful white handkerchief from his pocket and dabbed his forehead. Both his handkerchief and his extended pinky reminisced of a late eighteenth century gentleman's pose.

"Yes, I see." He surveyed the full benches, people sitting on the ground and others standing in groups. He dabbed his forehead again.

Haiti is frozen in time, I thought. *It won its independence in 1804, and receiving no help with governance, it simply modified and overlaid the slave-master society, the pecking order. Even gestures with the handkerchief remain the same.*

I smiled. "You have a full day before you, Messieur."

Walking to the edge of the large yard, I sat on a boulder by a stream.

Following her nose, Shelley peered over a fence to check out a homemade rum still. Coming back, she said, "More interesting over there."

The arbitrator divided the peasants into groups of twelve and presented them with a list of written questions for their discussion.

However, *su-preeze*, the farmers couldn't read.

Consequently, the poor man raced from group to group, circling, reading questions aloud and taking notes. He never loosened his tie.

Shelley played by the fence with two toddlers, a little boy with a swollen belly and a small girl with red hair. Playing chase, she caught the little boy, lifted him up and nuzzled his cheek. He squealed in glee.

I pressed my hand to my mouth.

When the arbitrator returned to his little table, he asked the crowd, "Do you want so-and-so to return as your manager of the farmers' Cooperative?"

A resounding "NO!" answered.

To the cheers of the crowd, the arbitrator ruled in favor of the Cooperative. The surly former manager was ordered to return the accounting books. Yet in Haiti, keeping peace is vital to prevent revenge; therefore, the cooperative was ordered to pay the manager a token sum.

I rocked to and fro, sighing relief and giving thanks.

Lisette, the Mother-Child Health Coordinator, asked me to come forward, and as I did, a farmer in a fresh straw hat and crisp shirt came forward, also.

"Madame Charlotte, our children are hungry," he said, gesturing to the audience. "The price of food is too high. We need a program that will feed our children."

I slowly rubbed my palms and spoke kindly.

"I know you are in hard times. You've made this request before. As Hans explained, the policy of our organization is to work with you in development. We do not fund food programs. I'm sorry."

Silence hung like wet drapery as the Coordinator translated my every word.

The farmer continued. "You are a new director. Do something for us. Help our children."

I looked at Shelley and the children with red hair and swollen bellies. If my child had symptoms of severe malnutrition, what would I do?

I cleared my throat as my eyes teared. "I'll research a program, but I cannot promise you success. Our organization does not grant food programs."

Touched by the gravity of their situation, I added, "I'll do my best."

With a pickup truck full of Haitians returning from the market after the afternoon rains, we headed for Le Jeune. A low, muddy strip of road oozed under the truck's weight and gave way. Like gliding on ice, we slid until a rear tire anchored in a shallow ditch.

Holding their shoes and pants or skirts high, Haitians clambered over the sides. I removed my shoes, slipped into the mud and pushed the door and wheel.

No movement.

"We need to rock the truck free; you'll need to push from your side, Shelley."

Shelley kicked off her shoes and angled her body against

the truck. Two well-dressed Haitians joined us as I climbed into the driver's seat.

Mud flew.

When we broke free, Haitians cheered the rewarding drama and leaped again into the rear.

Shelley moved the rearview mirror and looked at her face. "I'm covered with mud!"

She rubbed mud on her nose and cheeks and looked at her mud-soaked clothing. Reaching over, she wiped a streak of mud from my arm, and I pulled mud from her hair.

We laughed the rest of the way to Le Jeune.

"I get the shower first," she said as I pulled in front of the cabin in which we were staying.

"Not if I beat you!" I shouted, jumping to a head start.

We bounded from the truck, mud spattering from our heels, and raced toward the cabin.

CHAPTER SEVEN

"Remember the rain that made your corn grow."

— HAITIAN PROVERB

How odd that Shelley and I found a sense of family comfort against a backdrop of increasing violence. We reached a status of normalcy, or at least normalcy for life in Haiti.

A sense of balance returned, and I felt genuine happiness, a feeling of joy in my gut that had eluded me for years. With my contentment came hope. Joseph Campbell said something about when your inner world resonates with your exterior world, you can experience "the rapture of being alive." That brief period of time gave me that gift.

Shelley attended school and completed her homework without fuss, played on the tennis team and joined her friends after school.

I attended language classes, distributed the daily allotment for meals to a growing number of boys, focused on operations, launched two women's microenterprise programs, and began shaping a proposal for a children's feeding program for the Central Plateau.

In early evening, we drove to the Hotel Villa Creole where Shelley met friends, and I laughed with my Round Table of manufacturers. We kept track of political gossip, related humorous episodes that only Haiti can offer, always with mellow jazz playing in the background.

Home again, we lit kerosene lamps and shared our day. If we had electricity or used the inverter, we might watch a movie video.

The *timoun nan lari-yo* pursued their own routines. Lynx Air and the grocery store were prosperous targets. Both catered to internationals, Lynx Air for mail and the corner grocery store for specialized foods, such as American cheese and hot dogs.

The boys lingered nearby or sat on the sidewalk, and when a *blan* pulled into a parking space, they corralled the person or tapped on windows, always pleading *"mwen *ginyin yon pwoblem*" or "I'm hongry, Madame." Whoever received an occasional coin dashed off, one of the day's winners.

Shelley pumping purified water

During slow times, they wandered around Petionville, always on the prey for a good mark. Wherever, they constantly socialized. This included telling stories and playing jokes on one another.

Their community reflected the usual human relations found in concentric circles. In the center were Family (if they had any) and best friend (if they had one). Next, probably five trusted friends who slept together at night. An additional five or ten extended in a larger, but fairly close social group. Some of those might join the smaller group in sleep areas. Next, regardless of age, came the larger circle of acquaintances who lived in the Petionville area, and finally, the recognition of one street boy to another regardless of location.

Yet, as with life, interruptions occur, and for the *timoun nan lari-yo,* the underbelly of street life often brought catastrophic events. Adrien and his shaved head. Henri. Lucas. Pierre and the twins.

Waiting in front of Presse Evangelique, the twins held Henri's hands, his head cast down. In silence, one thrust a prescription toward me. Henri moaned and pulled his hands free to hold his head.

"What happened?"

"Henri was in a fight, and his enemy threw battery acid in his eye."

When Henri looked up, I gasped. Putrid yellow pus spilled from the injured eye.

"Have you seen a doctor?"

Henri covered his eye and pointed toward the prescription.

"How much is it?"

As usual, the prescription cost was more than the doctor's

visit. I quickly passed the money and told the twins to take him immediately to the pharmacy.

After my language lesson two days later, the boys came with Lucas in tow.

In a fight, his opponent had used a broken bottle and opened Lucas's shoulder in an eight-inch gash. A kind *marchand* had attempted to sew the wound with basting stitches of dirty thread. Between the stitches, the exposed wound hosted a legion of dirt particles.

The boys clustered about and stared at the serious injury. Fidgeting, they exchanged nervous looks while I turned Lucas and examined the wound.

Pierre made the sign of tetanus. He locked his jaws and stiffened his body, then shook as if in a death spasm. A few nodded; others shuddered. They had seen these kinds of assaults before. And deaths as well. It could happen to any of them, and if so, who would care?

My head spun.

When I told Lucas I would take him to a medical clinic, waves of motion and noise surged. After all, this was the first time Madame Charlotte permitted a *timoun nan lariyo* to ride in her machine. Such excitement! Their dream would be fulfilled; they would ride in the red machine!

They pushed and shoved, and a couple were already crouched in the cargo area.

"STOP!" I shouted as I pulled them out. "No one goes but Lucas."

A few looked hurt, like Mother had just told them they couldn't have candy, particularly Pierre who immediately sulked.

To Lucas, I said, "You can take one person."

"Adrien, I want Adrien."

We drove to a nearby green and white medical clinic that I passed daily and where I had observed poorer patients entering. Inside St. Germaine's, a stout nurse in a starched white uniform sat at a wooden school desk in a dark room.

No electricity, I thought. *A medical clinic and no electricity*.

After examining Lucas's shoulder, she said, "He'll need tetanus shot medication and antibiotic ointment. There's a pharmacy across the street. Go there; buy the medications and come back." For less than the costs of the medication, the nurse cleaned Lucas, stitched him and gave him the tetanus shot.

While the two boys walked toward the exit, the nurse took me aside and handed me the antibiotic ointment.

"He must keep the wound clean, but that isn't going to happen," she said, nodding toward the street. "He needs someone to clean the wound and change the dressing in several days."

I remained silent.

Her riveting eyes said it all. *Will the nicely dressed blan madame attend the wound of a dirty street boy, child without mama?*

At the machine, I handed the ointment to Lucas and relayed the nurse's instructions.

Two days had passed when Lucas appeared. Since the injury, he had not worn a shirt. His perfect, white teeth were striking against his iridescent ebony skin. Dirty gauze and tape dangled from his shoulder, held only by a smidgeon of tape.

I tried to re-arrange the hanging gauze with portions of tape and shuddered at the encrusted filth. When I chastised him, he answered, "The shirt hurt."

"Have you used the ointment?"

Of course not.

"Lucas, you've got to clean it and use the ointment, or it will become infected."

On the third day, Henri arrived. His shrunken eye sealed shut and dripping horrid pus. He pressed his temples, doing anything to stop the pain.

"The ointment didn't work."

"You need a doctor. I'll call a friend. Meet me here at four o'clock."

Taking a deep breath, I thought of Lucas. Turning to Adrien and Pierre, I muttered, "Find Lucas. Have him here at four o'clock, too. Tell him to bring the ointment."

Later, while driving to pick up Shelley, I thought, *I'm crossing a line, and once crossed, I cannot go back. I can always stop giving money, but once I take responsibility for tending their medical injuries—oh my!*

My counter thoughts clearly argued *if the kid isn't going to clean his wound, that's his problem.* Or, *being glassed on the street is a part of street life.* Those thoughts were blown away when I asked myself, *"What would God have me do?"*

When I picked up Shelley, I explained my plan to take Henri to see an ophthalmologist I knew in *la ville* (downtown), and while there, change Lucas's bandage. "I'll drop you at the Hotel Villa until I get back."

"Nope. I'm going with you."

I protested. "*La ville* is unpredictable. You know that. You never know when there's a strike or what's happening down there."

"I can help."

I chewed my lip. She could be a navigator. "Here's a map and some directions."

At four o'clock, we descended from the treed hills of Petionville to squalid streets, holding our noses as we passed open sewers, and entered *la ville*, the central area near the port where thousands came and went daily.

While I parked, Shelley retrieved the plastic gloves and bag with bandages from the glove compartment. We climbed the stairs to the second floor where the doctor's reception area held a number of straight-back wooden chairs.

Henri sat to wait his turn to see the doctor. Shelley and I took Lucas to an empty alcove down the hall.

"This is going to hurt. I'll be as fast as possible."

Lucas braced himself against the wall. With the first drops of hydrogen peroxide, he blanched. While I swabbed the dirt with cotton balls, he pushed against the wall, his brows knitted, and teeth clenched.

"I've never seen so much dirt! What have you been doing? Rolling on the ground playing soccer?"

He tried to smile, but couldn't unclench his teeth. I worked faster, but the dirt, ground deeply into his skin and stitches, resisted.

"You're hurting him, Mother. Stop."

"I have to clean it, Shelley." I extended my hand for another cotton ball.

"This is the last one," she said.

Throughout, Lucas never uttered a word.

The enduring Haitian. The Haitian who withstood lashings from the whip in much the same position as Lucas now was. Lashings that could open a back similar to the wound from a broken bottle. Like his ancestors, he never cried out.

When the wound was freshly bandaged, I gave Lucas the keys to the machine and a few *gourdes* to buy food from the *marchands* on the street. "*Pataje la mange.*" (Share the food.) Rest in the machine."

When Henri came from the examining room, he said, "It's too late. I'm blind. Where's Lucas?"

"Downstairs. He has some food for you." Squeezing his arm, I said, "Go on. I want to speak with the doctor."

The doctor's diagnosis was succinct. "He needs a corneal transplant to see again. I could do it, but we don't have donors or even the hospital instruments for that matter. You would be shocked to see what I operate with. At least I can take care of his infection and pain."

I thanked him for his kindness and opened my purse.

"No, Charlotte. You're not even Haitian and look what you're doing."

The numbers of street children, already gradually growing, increased dramatically. They chased my red machine and called my name wherever I was, even on the outskirts of Petionville.

In Petionville, street boys mobbed the "red machine" and blocked traffic. When I came from a building, a few beat on five-gallon tin cans with sticks while a few others chanted or danced. Enjoying the street drama, the women *marchands* selling vegetables bent in laughter.

However, not everyone thought we were worthy entertainment. When I approached the stairs of Lynx Air, Messieur Hate, the first *attaché* I had encountered, no longer sneered or laughed. He simply stared in an observant way. After that, I became aware of being observed by other *attachés*, men wearing generous shirts.

Pierre and Adrien again began calling me *"Mama,"* which I promptly refuted. *"Grunmoun,"* I reminded them, a wise, elderly person.

Teasing me about being *grunmoun* always tickled them, and therefore, we engaged in several re-enactments. This included a little pushing or dancing. After all, re-play doubles the entertainment value.

On a Sunday afternoon, Shelley and I decided to purchase soda pop. After several boys chased our machine, I drove further to a small store on the edge of Petionville. As we opened the cargo door and placed the sodas, I heard a woman say, "Look! There's Madame Charlotte."

I turned to see a mother and a little girl in pigtails dressed in her Sunday best, a pink sateen too big for her.

When the mother reached me, she shyly said, "Madame Charlotte," and warmly clasped my extended hand. Then she gently introduced her daughter. Taking her little hand, I replied, "It's nice to meet you." She beamed.

After they left, Shelley put her head on the SUV. "Good grief, Mother, they don't know you, but they know you."

CHAPTER EIGHT

"Love gives life within."

— HAWAIIAN PROVERB

The traffic slowed until it came to a complete halt. Since we trailed a large, bob-truck filled with standing passengers, I could not see the cause for delay. Opening the door, I got out for a moment to look ahead.

"It's a roadblock."

"Can we turn around?"

"No. The Round Table says never turn around. They'll shoot. Always go through a roadblock."

The truck eased forward. We followed. Two policemen ordered everyone out of the truck. They separated the men from the women and children and proceeded with individual searches.

"What are they doing?" asked Shelley.

"They're looking for someone in particular or searching for guns. Maybe both. Trouble is brewing today."

The policeman motioned me to pull alongside the truck. I handed him both Shelley's and my passports.

"Where are you going?"

"To the beach."

He read aloud, "Charlotte Wright," and studied my photograph and face.

His superior officer shouted and called him over. The officer returned the passports and waved us through.

We soon reached the outlying community where Baptiste, my tutor, lived. He had invited us for lunch, followed by a swim at a nearby beach. In addition to teaching, Baptiste was pastor of a small church, and we looked forward to meeting his family.

The private beach was unlike other beaches designed for

the Haitian elite and international set. This small beach curved around a quiet bay inlet and catered to middle class Haitians.

No lulling waves, no rivulets of Caribbean blue, no swirls of turquoise, only a too-warm, fuscous murkiness. The minimal waves and tides lacked the power to carry out human waste and trash. Despite years of living in Hawaii, I'm a terrible swimmer, and consequently, I swallowed some of the water. I wanted to retch.

Leaving Baptiste's house, Shelley reminded me that I promised to teach her how to drive a stick shift. I clicked my tongue while mentally calculating the distance remaining on the dirt road before reaching the highway.

We switched places.

"No, no, ease out the clutch. That's it, slowly, and ease on the accelerator. That's it. Oops, almost. Start the engine. Try again."

The machine lurched and sputtered, died, and lurched as we laughed our way to the highway where we switched places again.

By the time we reached Carrefour, I was really sick. "It must have been the water."

I stepped on the accelerator.

Driving on the shoulder, I passed lines of swaying tap-taps, then sped past five or six vehicles in a single effort, blowing the horn. I needed to reach home before the coming diarrhea. With virtually no traffic, I chose a shortcut through *la ville*.

"Something's up," I said. "Saturday and no traffic."

We arrived home with the setting sun.

In the bathroom, while I retched, pools of blood formed on the tile floor and sent a shock of fear through me. I felt the fire of my fever and knew I was in peril.

While Shelley went for ice and water, I splashed in the sink and drenched my body.

When Shelley brought the ice, she saw the blood on the floor. "What's that? That's blood!" The panic in her voice rose as fast as my fever. "Call an ambulance."

"There aren't any working ambulances."

"What?" she screamed. "No ambulances! Call the neighbor!"

I drank the water and wrapped the ice in a thin towel.

"She's gone." Our lone neighbor and landlord had moved to the United States until the political climate settled.

"Arthur!" But Arthur had already come and was standing behind her.

"I need to go to the hospital, but it's too hard to find. Anyway, I can't drive. Call the Villa and ask Marcia to bring help."

Shelley slammed the phone down in my bedroom. "It's dead!"

I put the thermometer in my mouth again. When it hit one hundred and five degrees, Shelley jerked it from my mouth, as though its removal would stop the climbing fever.

She tossed her head down, her hair cascading, and cried, "I don't know what to do, Mother!"

"Can you drive to the Villa? If you can't, I'll try." Inwardly, I knew I might pass out.

"I don't know, I don't know."

There are no safe choices, my little one.

"Arthur will go with you."

Arthur's eyes bulged. He lit the kerosene lamp.

"You can do this." Tears welled up within me as I iced my head and drank water again. "Find Marcia. She'll know what to do. If she's not there, ask the manager to find a doctor."

She left the room crying to get the car keys.

Arthur held my hand.

"I wish you knew how to drive," I whispered. "Protect her. It's a dark night."

Shelley returned with panic still in her voice. "The left turn, Mom? What about the left turn? What if the car dies?"

"Start it again." The left turn was made onto a major arterial avenue, and on nights with trouble, the streetlight would be out.

"Just remember. Ease out the clutch slowly and gently ease on the accelerator at the same time. You did it this afternoon. You can do it again. Keep control of the steering wheel."

She leaned down and stroked my burning forehead. "Mama, Mama, will you be all right? Promise me, promise me."

I promised.

Through my bedroom window, I saw twilight ending. Electricity was out on that Saturday night. That meant the *attachés* in white Toyota trucks would be on a killing spree.

Dear God, help her, protect her! Help her! Please.

I cried listening to the car lurching and sputtering down our little road. *Bon courage, my little daughter.*

My parched mouth absorbed every sip of water and still remained parched. I crawled to the bathroom. Pulling up to the sink, I dampened towels in cold water and crawled back to bed. Wrapping my body in the towels, I poured ice over my head.

The room darkened more, and shadows from the kerosene lamp hung like harbingers of death. I thought I saw Death lurking in the corner by the ceiling.

"Dear God, let me live. Please. Let me live. Help me, help me. Help her."

Verses from Psalms floated through my mind like lifebuoys upon a churning sea.

Guard my life and rescue me, for my hope is in you.

I clung to the memory of my father. When he was twenty-five, his appendix burst, and gangrene set in. The doctor told him he was dying. He prayed.

My mind drifted to his favorite, Psalm 91. *He will cover*

you with his feathers, and under his wings, you will find refuge.

I pictured myself resting in God's palm, and my breathing came easier.

Dad promised God that if he were allowed to live, he would serve Him and attend church as long as he was physically able. In a featured Christmas article, the St. Louis Post-Dispatch acclaimed him as the *"Good Samaritan of Southeast Missouri."* He spent his life helping those less fortunate. He taught Sunday School and often served as a lay minister. Robert William Foster never missed a Sunday service for fifty-four years.

I prayed through wandering thoughts mingled with random verses.

Where's Shelley?

You will not fear the terror of the night.

I held the image of Shelley's precious face before me, and in so doing, held on to life.

A grinding engine of a jeep and several other vehicles stirred me.

Heavy footsteps echoed on the stairs followed by Shelley's light, running feet across the living room tile.

She bounded into my room, triumphantly announcing, "I brought the United States Military."

Two men in civilian clothing entered. One said, "I'm a medic with Special Forces. Let's have a look."

He checked my fever, pushed on my stomach and lifted me to a sitting position. "We just arrived today, and I have no medications. Think you can make it to the hospital?"

"Special Forces?"

We're the advance logistical group. The Colonel's in the living room."

Marcia leaned in and said, "I have a couple of friends with me. We'll drive you to the hospital."

They carried me down.

"Sorry, it took so long," Marcia said as she helped me into their SUV. "There was a big strike today, lots of shooting in *la ville*. The U.S. government ordered us housebound. I had to get permission to leave the hotel, and the Special Forces escorted us here."

We wound down a deserted John Brown Avenue. Both Shelley and Marcia continued to wipe my head and give me water.

Suffice it to say that the hospital overnight stay was a

nightmare story no one could make up. In the morning, the doctor announced that according to blood results, I was gravely ill, possibly from e-coli or shigella. "Did I want to remain the hospital?"

No. I was alive and going home.

CHAPTER NINE

"Every river carries its own gravel."

— HAITIAN PROVERB

At home, I rested for a week. I suppose as with all near-death experiences, I reminisced of better times. Footsteps echoing through our home. Years as chief chauffeur for soccer, movies, parties. Halloween lunacy. Christmas warmth and joy.

I probed my decision to come to Haiti and put Shelley through such horrors as my illness. I began to think we should leave Haiti. Certainly, my health warranted the trip home. Like a vulture circling the heart of a matter, Mary's comment re-circled in my head, "Think about why you *really* came to Haiti."

Bedridden, I had plenty of time to contemplate why I came to Haiti. Flight was an easy pattern, a pattern I sometimes implemented when faced with situations I wanted to change. But that was not why I had come to Haiti.

I had run from teaching into marriage with a man I knew for a total of a week. The '60's. It seemed logical at the time. Surprisingly, the marriage lasted almost twenty years and produced three remarkable children.

I ran from the divorce to Washington State, a dream state for me with its rich foliage and damp skies. Although real estate was fruitful, I wasn't personally happy. The emptiness I felt reflected sadly and increasingly in my daughter's demeanor.

Three situations occurred within a period of five months to change our lives forever. Some call that intersection of events a perfect storm. I call it God's interventions.

The first situation began in late November 1992. I discovered my recycling and garbage were strewn about the yard. At first, I thought dogs were the culprits, and I placed heavy rocks on the lids of the bins.

No matter. I found discarded Christmas cards and other mail rummaged and tossed about. An instinctive fear crawled inside me, a primal feeling that caused me to look over my shoulder as I retrieved cards of good wishes for the coming new year. I did not yet know that going through discards was a behavior trait of a stalker.

The second situation was a call from the Middle School Principal in early February 1993. February! She notified me that Shelley would not likely be promoted to ninth grade. We met.

"I drop her off every morning. Where is she?"

The Principal didn't know. However, Shelley most likely would not be promoted from the eighth grade. She introduced this jarring news by saying, "Shelley doesn't show up, and she's radically short of the State's attendance requirements. It's doubtful she has time to make up the shortage."

"Please tell me how she earns A and B grades."

I waited for Shelley at our dining table. She came in as usual, slung her backpack and started for her room when I said, "Sit down." I patted the seat next to me. She chose the other end of the table, peering around the flower arrangement like a lost waif.

When I gave her the news about failure to promote, it was like the end of her world had finally arrived. First, we had shock, then shouting, "They can't do this!" magazine-throwing, and finally, collapse. All the pent-up depression, grief from family and divorce, frustration with frequent moves, lack of friends and place, racked her little body in gut-wrenching crying.

Overcome with guilt and my own sadness, I thought what a rotten mother I had been for the situation to reach such despair. I desperately wanted her to find a glimmer of hope.

What I ultimately had to say can be summed up in three sentences.

"Where do you go?" (The university coffee shop and bookstore)

Fidgeting.

"Do you really want to go to a school where you don't show up and still get "A's" and "B's"?

Silence.

"You should be flunking."

Stunned.

Meanwhile, the stalker grew bolder. With increasing frequency, I found a patio chair positioned to face the sliding glass door of my bedroom. Then other patio chairs were thrown about.

Answering my own questions of "Did I place it there?" "Did someone from the hot tub place it there?" concluded with finality, Stalker. Once, Shelley's bedroom screen had been removed and lay on the ground. I immediately replaced it. I began to triple check locks. Yet several times, the door from carport to kitchen was unlocked, and I consciously had locked it.

The third situation occurred on a Sunday morning in late February 1993, in the middle of the stalking dilemma and after the school revelations.

I insisted my rebellious fourteen-year-old daughter attend church with me in a nearby community where we had lived before. Arriving, we discovered we were an hour early. What a surprise; I'm rarely early. This was not a mistake of the alarm clock or daylight savings time. Weirdly, we had arrived an hour early. I must have misread my bedside clock, the kitchen clock and my watch. All three.

Bewildered, I suggested we explore the empty halls of Sunday School. We naturally gravitated to read the oversized bulletin board.

In the upper left corner was a thumbtacked job offer for a Field Director of Haiti for Development. As I read it, a memory stirred. Eighteen or twenty years prior I attended a special Sunday service that focused on Christian international efforts to combat world hunger.

I had always longed to do development work. I had the background for it, and I almost cried with yearning. *My children are so little*, I thought, *this won't be in my life.* At that moment, I felt a quiet reassurance, like a loving hand on my shoulder, and an angel of thought saying, *Your time will come.*

I stood before that typewritten job announcement and silently asked God, *Is this it?* Yet inside, I resisted.

Haiti? No, I don't think so. Somewhere in Latin America, maybe. After all, I have some Spanish, no French. Having given God my requirements, we turned and started back. Midway, I stopped. Why not jot down the information?

Next, Shelley and I were going away for a weekend, and I asked a friend to check the house. It snowed. Upon our return, the friend said, "You've got a problem."

A man's large footprints had left continuous circles around the house and on the patio, creating a visual picture of his frustration. Long strides. Probably 6'3" or so.

As too often occurs with single women, the police assume it is imagination. Or as one told me, "until someone is actually hurt [killed?], there is nothing we can do."

I launched my own search. In our extensive backyard, I found two tucked away areas with views of the house and my bedroom. The stalker had created camouflaged areas by arranging cut tree branches. Several beer cans lay there along with Marlboro cigarette butts.

I pondered and prayed for guidance.

The next time I asked Shelley to sit at the dining table, she sat beside me.

"You know, your life's not going well now, and neither is mine. What do you think about going overseas?"

"Like where?"

"What about Haiti?" I reminded her of the job posting on the Sunday School board.

She looked startled. "Isn't that where they have voodoo?"

"Yes, and honestly, the State Department has issued travel warnings. But if I get this job, the organization would take care of us, and if something went crazy, the Embassy would get us out. I won't apply unless you agree, and I may not be selected. If I'm not chosen, I'll look for something else, but only if you are willing."

As Shelley researched Haiti and related her findings, her excitement grew. She said it would be an adventure. After researching schools, we opted for a private high school where diplomats and internationals usually enrolled their children.

I felt hope rising for both of us. As I continued to ask for God's purpose, Isaiah 52:7 repeatedly appeared.

"How beautiful on the mountains are the feet of those who bring good news, who proclaim peace, who bring good tidings, who proclaim salvation, who say to Zion, 'Your God reigns!'" I began to wonder if that verse held relevance for me.

Meanwhile, I rented a trained German Shepherd police dog from Canada, and we patrolled the perimeter and the neighborhood at night. I discovered someone had shot out the streetlight on the street behind us, exactly aligned with rear entry to my yard. My flashlight shone on a pile of Marlboro cigarette butts and shattered glass.

A gnawing feeling of rejection settled as time passed and there was no word. Impulsively, I succumbed to an urge to call and inquire of the woman I had first spoken with regarding the job. She had not seemed eager to receive my application.

Expecting her voice, I was surprised to hear a man answer. The upshot was he was the International Director and was searching for something in her office at that moment. No, he had not seen my application, and he thought they had found a good candidate. I asked if he had seen my application. No. Looking around, he located my unopened FedEx package on a shelf.

A few weeks later, I was on the short list and in Grand Rapids, Michigan, taking psychological tests and completing interviews. I accepted the positiion while there. My immediate supervisor had arrived from Miami. When he picked me up for a gathering, his first words of disapproval regarding my selection rang harsh.

Since I had no desire to ask why, I simply replied, "I'm sorry, but I'm sure we will work well together."

In May, friends told me it wasn't too late to change my mind. On a particular night, several days before my scheduled departure for training, I awoke in panic at two o'clock in the morning. Quivering in cold fear, I decided I would not go. After all, my supervisor wanted someone else, and I could say I changed my mind.

Then a truly bizarre thing happened. I heard a voice in my head say, "Read Isaiah 61." Unfamiliar with Isaiah 61, I thought I must be crazy, but I turned on the light. I recognized that the verses spoke about Jesus Christ, and I saw no direct relation to me.

"He has sent me to bind up the brokenhearted...to comfort

all who mourn...to bestow on them a crown of beauty instead of

ashes, the oil of gladness instead of mourning, and a

garment of praise instead of a spirit of despair."

I had no idea what that meant for me. Still, I cried and knew that God wanted me to go to Haiti.

So, lying in bed recuperating, I grasped that in being a blessing for others, I was becoming a blessing for Shelley and myself.

As my body healed, I was healing within as well. I came to Haiti to fulfill God's purpose, which is often intricately woven.

Life returned to our Haitian normalcy, except with even less electricity, more violence, and excellent surprises.

On one such occasion, I stood at the top of the stairs of Lynx Air Office and called to the boys waiting below.

"I need four boys to help with boxes. Henri, Adrien, Pierre and Lucas. Come up."

When I entered the office of Lynx Air, several internationals looked askance, and the manager said, "Madame, we cannot have street boys in here."

"They're carrying boxes for me."

She stared over my shoulder.

I turned to see nine boys crowding the doorway.

"No!" I shouted. "I said only four. The rest of you go downstairs."

They dallied. After all, they might miss out on participating in something.

"Go. Now!" As they left, I apologized to the manager. She returned to her work without speaking.

"Two boys to a box," I said.

As the four boys shoved the two large boxes into my machine, Pierre grinned mischievously.

"Madame Charlotte, what's in the box? Something for us?"

CHAPTER TEN

"The horse knows the length of its rope."

— *HAITIAN PROVERB*

Circling the Hotel Villa Creole a second time in search of a vacant parking space, I mumbled, "This place looks like a used car lot for SUV's." Outside, chauffeurs huddled, smoking cigarettes, passing time until their international clients returned. I circled again and located a space in the hinterlands.

As I trudged toward the hotel, I thought about the arrival of the U.S. Special Forces advance group and the implementation of the brokered United Nations' Accords.

The Haitian military leaders finally had agreed to a specific October date to relinquish power and permit democratically elected President Aristide to return and assume the Presidency. There was a plan for amnesty for the *coup d'etat* leaders, and the U.S. Marines would arrive in mid-October to ensure a peaceful transfer of power.

Afterward, Haiti was promised a bonanza of development monies from the United Nations, the World Bank, U.S. Aid, and Canada. Ka-ching. Ka-ching. These monies would fund a re-organization of the military and police force along with new economic developments.

In other words, hope was dawning for the poorest country in the Western Hemisphere. Bingo. Haiti enjoyed a sudden influx of officials, their cars, their chauffeurs, and their plans about participating in a change of regime.

I even got caught up. Electricity. Hot water. Hot showers, oh my goodness. Working telephones. No more killing sprees of the *attachés*. No embargo. Affordable food for our families on the Central Plateau. Good begging opportunities for the *timoun nan lari-yo*.

Yet apart from Marcia and other U.S. Aid workers, the Round Table did not join in the high expectations.

That evening, Paul, owner of a trucking company, was in his cups. Loving Haitian rum, he was often in his cups, but he knew what was happening. "I don't care what the Accords say. We know the military won't step down. They'll pull the Haitian stall tactics."

Bill and Liz nodded in silence.

I surveyed the crowded restaurant and bar. With so many high-pitched conversations, I could barely hear the mellow jazz. Across the room, I spotted a table of ten men in shorts and tank tops. The medic from the U.S. Special Forces who had come to my home was among them. He saw me, and we waved.

Liz elbowed me. "Do you know them?"

"Not really. Where's Marcia?"

"With all of this activity, probably working late."

Such glumness amid all this gaiety.

"We've got a new microenterprise program for women in *Cite Soleil*." It was a special program designed with our missionaries and their church efforts in the worst slum in the Western Hemisphere. I was excited.

No one was interested.

Finishing another rum, Paul slurred, "It'll never happen. They'll stall, and we'll have civil war."

"Not civil war, Paul," said Liz, raising her eyebrows.

"Might as well be. People murdering each other, taking revenge for real or imagined wrongs. Blaming it on politics."

The clinking of glasses and hum of lively conversation dominated the Hotel's ambience. Businessmen in suits, United Nations' employees, young girls from CARE, U.S. Special Forces, Royal Canadian Mounted Police, U.S. Aid consultants, Ambassadors — all networked from table to table. Like stygian shadows biding time, the Round Table's somber mood stood in stark contrast to the anticipatory air of prosperity,

Bill turned to Liz and asked, "How are your plans coming?"

"I've begun. How 'bout you?"

Bill pushed his glasses on his nose. "I'm underway."

Paul leaned across to them. "That's easy for you to do. Close the factories and leave. Me? I have trucks. Here in Haiti. I can't run off to Costa Rica or the Dominican Republic. I'm stuck."

"Let me get this straight," I said, waving my arm toward the whirring room. "While all of these people celebrate the good times to come, you two are closing your factories?"

"It takes time to close a factory, so we're starting now. We've been through it before, haven't we, Bill?"

"I'm looking for a place in the Dominican. When I close this one, it's gone. I'm not coming back again."

He sounded almost relieved.

"And you?" I asked Liz.

"Probably Central America. No more Haiti. Haitians are the best workers in the world, but the country's too unstable."

The waiter delivered another rum to Paul. He swigged and said to no one, "Those government people are fools. They don't know the Haitian culture, and they didn't ask our opinion."

"What about you, Paul? If I get my food proposal funded, I'll need trucks to transport huge quantities of food to the Central Plateau."

"Unlikely, Char. Food trucks are a target. They'll be attacked. In fact, you'd better start flying up there, not driving."

"I may not even write the grant. My boss hasn't consented."

Yet in our daily lives, I saw no apparent reason to concede to pessimism. We continued in our routines with an added boost of hopeful energy. One evening is etched in my memory, a turning point as I viewed it.

Shelley and Alex pushed papers around the dining table while I worked at my desk. I paused to listen to their debate about black holes and their joint class report.

Shelley speculated about what a black hole might really be, its role in the universe, and Alex said they had no proof. They decided to include scientific theories, but Shelley insisted they include their own theories as well. Alex asked if that was scientific. I suppose she thought so because she began to draw.

Shelley studies at dining table

My ears tickled at the dynamic tones in her voice, trilling like music as she fearlessly explored a new universe. No longer numb, my Shelley was alive! Curious! And looking forward. Hope realized.

I walked to the balcony, leaned on the rail and enjoyed a vivid sunset. Broad-brush strokes of reds and corals dressed the mountains and sea. Below lay Port-au-Prince like a lady concealed under an amber umbrella of dust and pollution. A well of contentment hummed through me.

When Alex left, I went inside.

"Sounds like an interesting project."

"Yeah, it is," said Shelley, stacking and clearing papers. "She's really a good science teacher. She's the new one from Canada."

I pulled one of the large boxes from the corner and proceeded to open it. "Do you want to help me sort clothes, make outfits?"

"Like what?"

"Check the size of the pants, find a similar size shirt that goes with it. Fold them. Put the smalls' over there, the mediums' here, and the large in that corner."

"Oh, look at this," she said, holding up a pair of Bermuda

shorts with loud tropical designs. "The Hawaiian tourist." Shelley dug through the clothing until she found a t-shirt that matched well. "This outfit looks like Pierre."

"What size is it?"

"Medium."

"It'll fit. Here, pin his name to the shirt and shorts and put them here."

She folded the shirt, biting her lip. "Mom," she said in a tone of I've-got-something-to-say-and-you're-not-going-to-like-it.

"What?"

"You've got to do something about those boys."

Waiting, I held up a pristine white, large t-shirt.

"They beg from me after school when I'm with my friends. It's embarrassing! Fleur gives me disgusting looks."

I stopped folding the shirt. "Tell them to leave you alone."

"I DO! And they still bother me! They follow me everywhere." She mimicked them. "'Mademoiselle Shelley, give me a little something.' Fleur was shocked. She said, 'They know your name, Shelley. They call you by name!'"

Inwardly, my Irish flared. *They know your name, and by calling it, they insulted Haitian royalty, the Morally Repugnant Elite.*

I said nothing. I said nothing because she was right. The boys were out of control. I had lost my boundaries.

Shelley held up a pair of men's jeans and fingered a tiny hole in the butt. She folded them and placed them on the large pile.

"How much money do you give them? How much?"

"I don't know," I said, feeling a shield of defense rise in my chest.

"MOTHER! How much each day? How many are you feeding now?"

"A lot."

"Yes, a LOT! And the numbers keep growing. Why? Because you're feeding them! Where's the end to it?"

Shelley tossed a folded shirt toward the growing pile in the corner. "Mom," she lectured, facing me squarely, "You're not rich. Can you afford to do this? The last I checked we don't have much money."

I rubbed my temple. *No, I can't afford to support the growing numbers.* "I'll set limits."

Shelley looked as though she would cry. "I feel awful saying this. I know they need help and food. I feel like a spoiled brat." She started to cry, then pleaded, "But Mom, I have friends! And you don't have the money!"

"You're not spoiled." I took her in my arms and hugged her.

At Presse Evangelique on the patio where I studied with Baptiste, I sought his advice. When I explained the chants, the chasing of my machine and mobbing me when I got out, he rested his head in his hands.

I studied him. Closely cropped hair, cinnamon complexion, straight nose, manicured nails. His starched, white shirt glistened as a breeze swayed the rubber plants beside him, permitting a ray of sunlight to wave across his slim body. Baptiste had substance.

He looked up. "What do you want to do?"

"I want them to choose a leader. I want the leader to have a list of names, and each day I'll give the leader the money for food. The leader will see that the boys whose names are on the list receive three gourdes each for a meal.

Baptiste stared in disbelief. He coughed, looking aside as though thinking how best to explain the situation to me. He opted for simplicity.

"Charlotte, these children are different. They're *timoun nan lari-yo*. From the streets. They don't cooperate with each other. They don't trust each other. They will not follow directions."

"I understand your view, but I think they can work together."

He took a deep breath and sighed. "It's more than that." His voice lowered. "These children are dangerous."

"No, no, I don't think so. I mean, they may let the air out of tires sometimes or steal things, but dangerous? No."

"Dangerous in another way." His voice sunk to a near whisper. "Politically dangerous. Father Aristide cared about these children and established several orphanages for them. They loved him, and on at least one occasion, they saved his life before an assassination attempt. The *attachés* hate them. During the *coup*, they burned an orphanage. The merchants hate them because they harass their customers."

We sat in silence for a moment.

"Do you still want to do this?"

"I have to do something. They're out of control. Will you translate for me?"

At noon the following day, we met with the boys in the park square. As the number of boys increased, the number of onlookers increased as well. Who knows? Someone may want to participate.

"Sit down," I said. "Everyone sit down."

No one sat. Baptiste glanced at me, saying *I told you so*.

"SIT DOWN!" I motioned them to the ground.

Amazed onlookers gaped at the surprising social order and moved in closer. Those in generous shirts kept their distance.

"I want you to select a leader."

Baptiste translated.

Blank stares.

"Every morning I will give the leader enough money for each of you to have a three-gourde meal. There are too many of you now. I cannot give to you individually. I'll give to one leader, and one only. He will provide for the rest of you. Who do you choose?"

Beginning looks of panic. Some noise and fighting broke out, and a few leaped to their feet.

I frowned.

Surrounding boys yanked on the arms of those standing and pulled them down again. "Shh—*respecte!* Madame Charlotte is talking."

I'm witnessing infant democracy.

Baptiste shrugged, ready to give up.

"All right, think about this. If you had to depend upon one person to make certain you eat, who would you trust?"

Noise and confusion rippled through the group.

"The leader will run off with the money," called Adrien. "He'll share it with his friends, and there will be nothing left for us."

Baptiste and I looked at each other. Taking care of oneself and friends had been the Haitian way since 1804. *Degage pa peche.* "It is not a sin to take care of yourself." How could we expect street children to behave differently and more honorably than their government leaders behaved?

I raised my hand in the air, shouting, "Quiet!"

Baptiste imitated my every tone and gesture. When I pointed for them to sit down, he did likewise, and they sat. When I raised my voice in drama, he did likewise.

A few in generous shirts came closer. While I knew guns

were under those shirts, my sense was they were more curious than threatening. I ignored them and continued with business at hand.

"I'm going to give one person, your leader, money for your food in the morning. He will have a list of your names. He must know how to write and read your name. During the day, he will give you each three gourdes for a meal. You'll have to find him. He's not going to find you."

"Madame Charlotte, what if the leader refuses to give us the money?" one called.

"You tell me." With exaggerated finger-waving, I uttered a severe pronouncement. "If he is not an honest leader, I will never, NEVER give him money again. Not even one gourde!"

"Ahh-aa," they muttered, looking to one another, satisfied with the dire consequences for a dishonest leader.

"Now who do you choose?"

A quick, unanimous decision was cast for Henri by a show of hands. Since Henri had completed third grade, he could read and print their names, however slowly.

I called Henri to stand before the group.

"Do you understand and agree to act with honor as their chosen leader?"

He nodded.

"Say 'I do.'

"I do."

"Will you distribute the money fairly as I've told you to do?"

He nodded, adding, "I do."

I handed a notebook and pencil to Henri. Then I put my finger in air, assuming a commanding manner.

"Wait. Before Henri writes your names, I have something very important to say."

An uneasy silence fell, and they looked one to another.

"No one, NOT ONE OF YOU, WILL BEG FROM MADEMOISELLE SHELLEY AGAIN." I pointed to my chest. "I'm feeding you, not my daughter. I pointed to them again. "You do not ask her for "a little something" anymore. You do not bother Mademoiselle Shelley at all. Do you understand?"

A few nodded.

"Listen well," I said with all the vehemence I could muster. "If you bother Mademoiselle Shelley, or her friends, again, I will strike your name from the list."

I pointed toward the notebook and struck an imaginary line through an invisible name. "You will never get money from me again. Do you understand?"

They quickly nodded, and Pierre made a slitting gesture across his throat. They understood perfectly.

"Good. Now, one by one, we'll go down the line. Call out your name when it's your turn. The rest of you be quiet while Henri makes the list.

Henri gripped the pencil like a kindergartner, and in large scrawl, he slowly printed the names of twenty-two boys present. But the list didn't stop. Boys continued to call out names of those absent.

"Dominique" was shouted.

I interrupted. "I don't know Dominique, and he's not here. He's not on the list."

"You know Dominique, Madame. He's as tall as Adrien and his hair is brown with curls." Pierre made circles around his eyes. "Green eyes."

"Oh yeah, Dominique."

The final list was a staggering thirty-seven boys, ages seven to sixteen. In the coming months, the list would grow to fifty. Henri folded his list like a treasure map and tucked it into his jeans' pocket. Everyone was satisfied, that is, almost everyone.

Pierre inched a finger upward for my attention. "Madame Charlotte, can we go to school? We want to read."

CHAPTER ELEVEN

"God says, 'You do your part. I'll do Mine.'"

— HAITIAN PROVERB

Since the new international fervor spilled into local restaurants, I was not surprised I had to park two blocks away from my corner pizza café on a Friday night.

I raced through the light rain to beat the imminent deluge. In the crowded café, I located a small table adjacent to the open doorway.

Like being seated at a performance, the cloud curtains opened, and the heavens rained. And rained. I had almost finished my meal when I heard, "Pssst, psst, Madame Charlotte. Madame Charlotte!"

At the door stood Pierre with several other boys. Water dripped from their noses, and clothing clung to their damp bodies.

Pierre's eyes sparkled like raindrops in light. He made the motions of eating and pointing to pizza, clapping his hands together without making a sound.

I smiled at his sheer delight in everything.

Walking over, I asked, "How many are here tonight?"

"Six."

The waiter shooed them away, and I returned to my seat, waving to the waiter. I ordered the largest combination pizza to go, cut into six pieces.

By the time the pizza arrived, the rain was blinding in its force. Water overflowed downspouts, and like a river following a gorge, currents sought the lower portions of concrete.

I was at the door when Pierre shouted "Wait!" He motioned for me to remain in the doorway. Running across the patio, barefoot of course, he dodged tables with closed umbrellas and leaped puddles.

The six boys returned with a heavy, large plastic sheet, undoubtedly retrieved from where they would eventually sleep. They held it over their heads, three on a side.

"Under here, inside," said Pierre, beaming, "You won't get wet."

I scampered to the center among them. Rain pounded the plastic, but the thick sheet held. I felt like the Queen of Sheba as the escorts led me to my machine. Completely dry, I slipped into the machine and carefully passed the steaming treasure to Pierre and his salivating group.

By morning, the rain clouds had passed, and the sunrise cast its rosy glow upon wisps of cotton.

The plane flight to Pignon will be clear, I thought, as I climbed into my usual co-pilot seat on the chartered single-engine plane. The drone of the engine whirred to the back of my mind as I thought about Shelley.

"You want to stay with Mateo's family?" I had asked in surprise. "I like his parents, so it's fine, but I thought you might stay with Marilyn."

"They have something going on, and Mateo's parents invited me. They have all kinds of things to do at their house."

I gave her *the look.*

"Mateo's just a good friend, Mom," and she meant it.

The little plane climbed higher as its belly skimmed over the first mountain range. Green trees and brown earth rose to greet us. As the plane wobbled in the mountain wind, the pilot reached over and maneuvered the stabilizer bar. Even here, at the top of Haiti's world, worn paths wound their way to thatched huts, and lazy charcoal smoke drifted upward.

We began the descent to the grass airstrip built by the U.S. Marines in 1919 after their invasion. The pilot leaned over and pointed down. Over the roar of the engine, he shouted, "We're going to fly low, make sure the airstrip is clear."

Several piles of oversized truck tires stacked with shrubbery lay scattered in the middle of the field. As we buzzed above the ground, Haitians hustled out and removed the tires and debris. We circled again and swooped down, hovering right over the ground."

"Just to make sure."

We made our final circle and touched ground.

"Why the tires?" I shouted as we bumped down the grassy strip.

"The Haitian military thinks the U.S. military will use this airstrip when they come in a few weeks, so they're booby-trapping it."

He turned the plane and taxied back to the middle.

I snorted. "An invasion? What about returning Aristide peacefully?"

"Who knows the Haitian mind? For me, today's a good day. No loose goats."

Following the meeting with all Coordinators, I sat with Lisette, the Mother-Child Health Coordinator. She wanted an update on our pursuit of the food program for the children.

"You know," I said, "we are a long way from getting this grant. First, my supervisor must agree, and so far, he hasn't. If he does, we have to write the grant proposal. Then, who is going to fund it?" The U.S. government won't allow money coming here.

She nodded, twisting in her hard-backed chair.

Grasping for a reprieve from this impossible subject, I said, "If President Aristide returns, the embargo will be lifted. We won't need this program."

Lisette chewed a different fingernail. "It takes a long time for the prices of food to go down." She wrinkled her nose.

"Who really believes General Cedras will allow President Aristide to return?"

I sat silently, thinking. *That's the grim prediction of everyone I know. Everyone, that is, except the U.S. and U.N. diplomats. The stacked tires on the grass runway confirm the Haitian stall is coming.*

"Okay," I said. "At least we can prepare. Start the research. Numbers of children, ages, mothers, locations, foodstuffs needed."

Lisette licked the tip of her pencil and began writing.

"And storage," I added. "If the military refuses to step down, the food situation will worsen, and food anywhere becomes a target. Where will you store the food and how will you protect it?"

She continued to write.

"This is not a promise, Lisette. Let me be clear on that. Don't raise expectations that this is going to happen. Let's just work on it privately."

I didn't voice the most critical challenge in my mind, assuming a proposal was funded. Although we could purchase some of the fresh vegetables at the marketplace, how would I transport tons of other foodstuffs, like cooking oil and rice, to the Central Plateau?

"Si Bon Dye vle," I added. (If God wills.)

Lisette repeated, *"Si Bon Dye vle."*

The little plane returned in early afternoon, as it must, so we could cross the mountains before clouds descended.

After picking up Shelley and refreshing at home, we went to the Hotel Villa. The Round Table gloom hung like a small cloud in the joyous atmosphere. Marcia was again working late.

"Look at the crowd out there," said Bill. "In three or four weeks, it'll be empty again."

I knew he was right. Soon the hotel would be as vacant as it had been after the U.N. announced its embargo on oil and guns. The government representatives, the opportunists, the profiteers, the do-gooders, the wanna-be's — all came and went with the political tides of fortune.

My begging street boys would face starvation. I wondered if I could afford a five-gourde meal.

"Perk up, Bill. It'll be all right." But it wouldn't be all right, and I knew it.

"Haiti's getting to me," he said. "Now every working Haitian supports seven people on a pittance, and soon it will be ten. Thousands will be out of work when the factories close, which we must do."

"Time for a change of subject, shall we?" prompted Liz. "What are you up to, Char?"

"Fun stuff actually. This Saturday Shelley and I are taking the street boys down to my office for some new clothes. *Bon rad*." (nice clothes)

"What?"

"Yep. Some friends sent boxes of clothing. Shelley and I've made an outfit for each boy on the food list and pinned his name to it. I'm going to take them down in groups, little ones first, then middle ones, and then the big ones."

Paul laughed. "How are you going to manage them?"

"Some men from the office will help. We're going to have an assembly line."

"Haitians in line?" guffawed Paul.

"No, that can't be. An orderly line?" added Liz.

I sipped my beverage. "Scoff if you want, but hear me out. One of the men will give each boy a towel when it's his turn and his set of clothes. He'll take a shower with soap! Then change into his new duds. I'll bring them back to the park and pick up the next group."

The Round Table chided me with disbelief. Even Bill chortled.

"Come on, get real," said Paul. "American Airlines in Miami placed the Port-au-Prince counter in an obscure area, so no one could see or hear the chaos." He raised his glass, waving for a busy waiter. "They hired special employees whose sole task is to ensure a fair line, and they still can't do it."

Haitians in line

Everyone laughed, for we all had experienced that disaster in Miami, another consequence of the embargo.

"I'll believe it when I see it," said Liz.

"I'll take photos."

"Yes, take pictures. We need proof you have Haitians standing in line."

CHAPTER TWELVE

"Life is a pair of split pants without suspenders."

— *HAITIAN PROVERB*

The boys paced the meeting area in the park like racehorses waiting for a starting gun. After all, they were finally going to ride in the machine! A dream comes true! The usual onlookers also had gathered and gradually surrounded us so they might hear what was happening. Perhaps they might want to join in.

Two older boys, one carrying a long stick, strutted across the grounds and stood at the fringe of the boys.

The one with the stick was Victor, the bullying boy at Lynx Air parking area. Today, Victor was swinging his stick like a weed whacker rather than cuffing the boys. I wondered what he intended, undoubtedly no good.

"No, no, no," I said, as the boys crowded and pushed, each wanting to be first into the machine's cargo area.

"The machine's locked, Madame Charlotte."

"Yes, I know."

"Where are the clothes?" asked Pierre, gawking through the window.

"At the office." I gathered the boys around. "Remember, the little ones first, ages seven to eleven. When I call your name, line up and climb into the rear." I unlocked and opened the door. "After this group gets their clothes, I'll bring them back and take the next group. Ready?"

Definitely. Wearing attractive, stylish, clean clothes is a core value in Haiti, regardless of income or status. *Bon rad.*

"Richard, Garry Jean, Louis…."

The youngest group went like clockwork. While they stood in line on the stairs, Shelley took photos. They giggled and smiled.

When we returned to the park, the excitement level increased.

"Ah, *bon rad*!" the boys exclaimed, fingering the pressed shirts and shorts of the returning group.

A grown man, an onlooker, tapped me on the shoulder and pointed to a small stain. He wanted to participate.

"I'm sorry for your need," I said, "but you're too big. I have only boys' clothing."

I read the names of the next group, ages twelve through fourteen. "Pierre, Adrien, Lucas, Charles--"

"Victor!" the strutting youth with the stick called. He pushed through the boys to the head of the line. His companion followed. "Victor and Ronald," he repeated, and he clambered into the machine, followed by his friend.

"I'm sorry; your name is not on my list. You're too old."

Ignoring me, he tapped his stick on the carpeted floorboard.

"Please get out."

"I'm going."

Shelley and I exchanged glances. She raised her eyebrows, saying *now what?*

"No. You're not going. This group is for boys twelve to fourteen. Are you fourteen, Victor?" I thought he was eighteen or nineteen.

His finely trimmed moustache twitched.

"Out!" I commanded, pointing firmly toward the park.

His companion scooted out and disappeared to the edge. Victor stared at me.

"Look at you. I'm sorry, Victor. You're too big, and you're not fourteen."

Slowly he emerged and stopped in front of me. "I'm out now, Madame Charlotte, but the next trip, I'm going." Erect and proud, Victor walked away, swinging his stick like a royal walking cane.

As we drove away, Shelley asked what we were going to do.

"Read the list of the bigger boys. See if anyone's absent."

"We have two spare sets of clothes, Mom."

"Size large?"

"No, but we can juggle some. Want me to do it?"

"Yeah. Work on that when we get there, before we give out the clothes to this group."

Above the chatter in the rear, Pierre asked, "Madame Charlotte, will Victor get new clothes?"

"I don't know. Who is he anyway?"

Adrien answered. "Victor's okay. He's on the street, too, just older."

"Why does he carry that stick?"

Adrien laughed. "He wants to be somebody, a big shot. He's okay, Madame."

Sweet Adrien sees the good in everyone.

When we returned, the group gathered around Pierre in his Hawaiian tourist outfit. Pierre posed and drew a comb from god-knows-where. Standing tall like a movie star, he dramatically swept the comb through his cropped hair.

"Mr. Suave, you're lookin' good," I said, giving him a thumbs-up.

He grinned.

When I pulled my list to call the names of the boys, ages fifteen through seventeen, Victor pushed to the front of the line again followed by his friend.

"Victor, you can come, but you cannot bring that stick."

He looked at the stick and fingered his moustache.

I began the roll call. "Henri, Claude, Philippe, Jean."

I paused to see Victor debating my request.

"No stick in my machine, Victor. Choose."

Victor hurried through the boys, dropped the stick and returned. "I'm ready, Madame Charlotte."

"Victor, Ronald."

When we arrived at the office, we reviewed the procedure.

"You'll take the new clothes and a towel. Then you'll shower, go to the private room and change. Victor and Ronald, you must be last. Afterward, Shelley's going to take your photo.

The elaborate need to pose slowed the picture taking. Resting a thoughtful finger on the cheek while the other hand supported a bent elbow was a favorite posture. Smiling was out of the question since a serious demeanor conveyed one's importance. These boys were especially important.

Afterward, Shelley and I sat in my office. She rested her head in her hands, exclaiming, "I thought we'd never finish."

"It went well, don't you think?" I felt warm and toasty, like sitting before a fire and sipping hot chocolate on a snowy day.

She grinned. "They like the *bon rad*, Mom."

"You did a terrific job in juggling those clothes. I was unsure what we could do."

While we congratulated each other, Victor appeared at the door.

"Madame Charlotte," he said sheepishly, *"Merci."*

"Victor," I said, trying to hide my surprise. "Come in. Let's see how the clothes fit."

With graceful confidence, he strode to the center of the room and turned around. Victor's childlike joy with his snug, white top and jeans with a tiny hole in the rear contrasted starkly with his usual fierce manner.

I sat silently, admiring the art of it all, his walnut muscles rippling against the smooth, white cotton and his genuine happiness with his new look.

"You look terrific, Victor. Hope you like it."

"I do. *Merci, merci."*

When he left the room, Shelley and I stared at each other, eyes popping and mutually mouthed, "Wow."

The Round Table passed the photos among them.

"Notice how straight the line is," I said.

"I'm impressed, Char. Didn't think you could do it," said Liz.

"We had money on this, didn't we? I'm sure we did."

Paul raised his glass. "Here, here. Haitians in line. You should run for President."

That night I lay in bed and listened to the beginning of the *Vodou* ceremony in the ravine, the call to Legba, the great *loa* (Haitian god) who controls the crossroads between the earthly and spiritual realms. Next began the songs or chants with *rada* drums or conches for certain *loas* to cross over from the spiritual world and ride them. To ride them meant for the *loa* to take possession of their bodies, and they entered a trancelike state.

Normally*, hounsi* (*Vodou* females) would sing, and we would hear the songs for Erzulie, *loa* of love or protector of women and children. Almost every Saturday we saw *hounsi* walking through town in their bright yellow and red sateens. The rhythm of the drums suggested the ceremony was a *rada* one, that is, a peaceful one.

But the ceremony that night was different. I leaned on my elbow and listened. These were *petro* drums pounding full of fury and violence. Instead of songs urging Erzulie to come, fierce chants and singing rose from the ravine. The heartiness reminisced of soldiers before battle, singing with barrel chests and proud hearts, persuaded of coming glory.

They're calling down the loa Ogoun, Haitian god of war. I took a deep breath and audibly blew it out. They weren't pleading for his intervention and protection. Their savage chants and gunfire commanded him to come down and ride.

I gasped at a sudden realization. It was common knowledge that historically, the paramilitary was steeped in *Vodou*. This ravine, our ravine, was the *Vodou* location for the *attachés*. The military fortress at the beginning of our narrow dead-end road also contained a solitary dirt road that lead from the fortress down the hill into the ravine. They had total protected privacy.

Messieur Hate and his thugs were probably there. I chewed my inner lip as his portrait of malice flashed, a sardonic smile with gold teeth.

I got up and walked to the jalousie bank of windows in the living room. It was dark and even if the lights had been working, I would not have been able to see through the oleander hedge at the cliff edge.

What kind of karma do I have? How did I select a house above the paramilitary's ravine?

As I returned to bed, I heard several generators click from

surrounding houses that lined the cliffs, but not sufficiently to drown the drums. An ominous feeling crept over me, like a spreading slick of black oil. If any doubt remained about the real intent of the military to prevent President Aristide's return, it was eliminated.

Evacuation may lie ahead for us, I concluded, thinking about Shelley. She was happy, finally finding herself, enjoying school and friends. I prayed, whispering the verse that came to me, Isaiah 30:21. *Whether you turn to the right or to the left, your ears will hear a voice behind you saying, This is the way; walk in it.*

Shelley came into the room. "Mom, what's happening? This isn't normal."

"I'm not sure," I said, opening the mosquito net. "Want to sleep here tonight?"

CHAPTER THIRTEEN

"Never curse the crocodile until you've crossed the river."

— *NIGERIAN PROVERB*

A cataclysmic event occurred at the Catholic Cathedral in *la ville*. A mass commemorating slain supporters of President Aristide was in session. In attendance was Messieur Antoine Izmery, a well-known and much beloved humanitarian who also was an outspoken critic of the military leaders.

During the service, policemen entered and dragged Messieur Izmery from the Cathedral into the street. They shot him and left his body for all to see, an unnerving lesson. The entire city was shocked.

Messieur Izmery's daughter attended Shelley's school, and Shelley was privy to her call to the office to learn the devastating news. Because Haitian revenge often extends to the family, the school went into lockdown complete with guards and M-16's.

Having never been exposed to such hatred and violence, Shelley was a wreck. She sat at the table and sobbed. And sobbed, repeating, "I don't understand. Why? Why?"

"It comes down to power. *Degage pa peche*. Whoever has the power has the money. Money to buy benefits for family and friends. Importance. Trips. Schools. Food. Everything. Whatever they want."

The American Embassy recommended all Americans stay home the day of Messieur Izmery's funeral in Petionville. We obeyed. From our balcony, we watched black smoke rise from burning tires in *Cite Soleil*, the horrendous slum filled with Aristide supporters.

At my next language lesson, Baptiste whispered chilling news. "After Izmery's funeral, two teachers outside of the Cathedral overheard a group of *attachés* discussing the anniversary of the *coup d'etat* that overthrew President Aristide. It's coming up, you know."

Yes, I knew. September 29 or 30, 1991. "Go on."

"In celebration of the *coup*, the *attachés* plan to kill the *timoun nan lari-yo* in Petionville on that date."

I gasped. "What? You can't be serious."

"Very serious. They asked me to tell you."

"Who are these teachers? How well do you know them?"

"They're credible. They're telling the truth."

"I can't believe the *attachés* would do that. Why?"

He leaned closer, his voice barely audible. "They hate the street boys, and so do the merchants. They hate them because the street boys saved Aristide's life, and the boys are a nuisance to the merchants and their clientele. October is always violent in Haiti. I don't know why. It can happen."

I tried to swallow, but my mouth was dry.

Baptiste looked away, then hurriedly added, almost as an afterthought, "They asked if you could do something to stop it."

"Me? I don't know. I don't know. I find this whole thing hard to believe."

We decided my best option was the American Embassy.

The American flag hung limply in a corner. Behind a very official desk, sitting in a very official black chair, the Embassy administrator twisted a very official plump, black pen trimmed with gold.

"So, you see, the American government can do nothing. Of course, if the street children are killed, we can raise the issue in the United Nations and bring international pressure to bear."

I resisted commenting on the complete fecklessness of international pressure to date. Shredding a tissue, I asked, "Do you believe this could really happen? Harm children?"

"It's possible."

"Why? I don't get it."

"Sacrificing children sends a strong message. It says, 'We are capable of doing anything.' They don't want to give up power, and they don't want an American invasion. This could be a strategy of instilling fear, making the United States think twice about responding if they reject the Accords. The boys are caught in the middle, and so are you, it seems."

I shredded the tissue into smithereens. "Do you have any suggestions? Advice?"

The representative cleared his throat. "You can remove them from the situation, from the city."

"To where? The provinces?"

He nodded.

"Many of them are not from the provinces, and many don't have families."

"Or," he paused, "You can do nothing."

"Nothing?"

He nodded. "Tell the boys about the plot so they can prepare themselves. Detach yourself. It's up to them what they do."

My heart fell like a house of cards. *There are no safe choices, Charlotte.*

For the next few days, I couldn't bring myself to say anything. I repeatedly prayed for God to show me the way. Every time I saw them, I saw their bright eyes and innocence. I pushed the horrible news away and prepared for the now eight-hour drive to Pignon on the Central Plateau.

Without notice, the men who were to accompany me returned to Pignon the day prior, Haitian style. Too late to get a charter plane, I would be driving that dangerous route alone. Canceling the trip was not an option. The Board had important items on its agenda, and the staff needed cash. Rural Haiti is a cash and carry economy.

What if I have a flat tire? What if I have two? What if I have trouble at the military checkpoints? What if I get robbed? What if I get sick? What if, what if?

The queue at the bank extended out the door to the stairs. A street boy, Nicolas, stood chatting with a uniformed security guard packing an M-16. I walked over to say *"Bonjour."* Looking at the growing queue, I said, "Wow. I'll be here for three hours, and I'm driving to the Plateau."

"Follow me," said the guard.

I followed him past the line, into the bank, across the lobby into a private room. He whispered to a woman behind a teller's barred window. *Voila!* I had my money.

Leaving the bank, I thanked him and extended my hand.

He shifted the M-16 and accepted the handshake. "You take care of Nicolas, Madame. I take care of you."

Nicolas grinned, a youth with reddish hair from bleach, not malnutrition. He waved to his friend and walked me to the parking lot.

Inspiration struck.

"Nicolas, what are you doing this weekend?"

He chewed his gum faster. "Nothing."

"Have you ever been to the Central Plateau?"

He shook his head, chewing his gum even faster.

"Do you want to go? We can take five boys in the machine."

"When?"

"Now."

Nicolas stopped chewing his gum. "Can I have fifteen minutes to get ready?"

"Meet me at Lynx Air. I'll round up the others."

CHAPTER FOURTEEN

"God knows how to put a crab in a blindman's sack."

— *HAITIAN PROVERB*

By the time Nicolas arrived, Pierre (Mr. Suave), Adrien (the gentle), Lucas (the wounded) and Rafel (the naïve) waited. Piling into the machine, they asked a flurry of questions.

"Where is Le Jeune?"

"What is a dormitory?"

"Will I really have a bed?"

"A toilet?"

"No-o-!"

"It flushes?"

"Madame Charlotte, you're joking."

"Is there a shower?"

"Can I shower?"

"With soap?"

I had backed out of the parking lot when Adrien shouted, "Stop, Madame, we need to take Martin."

I braked, glanced back at Adrien and then at Martin who sat on the steps of a building. Recently arrived from Cap-Haitien, Martin had come to try his luck on the streets of Petionville.

I rubbed my nose and said, "No, we don't need to take Martin."

Probably eighteen, Martin wasn't a youth planning to go bad so much as a boy waiting for bad to happen to him. I sensed a lack of backbone, and the cruncher was that he was a little too oily for my preferences.

"Pleez, Madame," said Pierre, tapping me on the shoulder. "Martin wants to go home."

"We're not going to Cap-Haitien."

"He can take a *tap-tap* (public taxi) to Cap-Haitien. It's close, isn't it?"

"It's close compared to Petionville."

"What does a ride matter?" asked Nicolas.

That said it all. What did a ride matter? There's always room for one more.

Adrien sealed the offer. "Madame, Martin isn't doing well. He needs to get off the streets."

I knew what that implied. If so, Martin needed to get off the streets .

"Someone's got to sit in the cargo area."

Pierre laughed and clambered over the seat.

Martin joined our entourage, and off we went, singing Haitian songs, laughing and teasing each other. I decided to wait about the rumor of *attaché* assassinations. *Let them enjoy themselves.*

When we reached the Mirebelais military checkpoint, the casual lieutenant with a cigarette hanging from his lips said, "Madame, the commanding officer wants to speak with you." He motioned toward the guard shack.

I didn't move. Never had I encountered a situation at this lackadaisical outpost.

The lieutenant gestured for me to get out of the car.

I told the boys to wait for me and assured them I would be right back.

"I'm going with you," said Martin, who was riding shotgun, the last-minute addition who got the best seat.

I started to protest, but Martin was already out of the car.

Inside, the commander icily inquired, "Where are you going, Madame?"

"To Le Jeune Mission, near Pignon."

"What is the nature of your business?"

I handed him my business card that usually was interpreted as a missionary. "I'm going to a Board meeting."

He asked where the boys were from and why they were traveling with me.

"They're *timoun nan lari-yo* from Petionville. I asked them to come. They'll stay at the dormitory at Le Jeune Mission."

Squarely facing me, he said, "Where is your chauffeur? All *blan* women have chauffeurs. Who are you that you drive yourself in the company of *timoun nan lari-yo*?"

A fearful ah-ha moment struck. To me, these boys were

children. To those in power, they represented a formidable foe. If trained, their youth and agility could form an army. A United Nations' study had projected at least three thousand *timoun nan lari-yo* lived in Port-au-Prince alone. Imagine an organized army of three thousand inside the City.

The commander wonders if I'm driving them to a training camp.

Adopting an obsequious manner, Martin eased into the conversation. Bowing, he leaned across the counter. In velvet deference, he said, "Madame Charlotte is a missionary, Sir."

Oil at its best.

"She takes care of the *timoun nan lari-yo* in Petionville. She buys them food every day, so they don't starve. She gives them clothes. She takes them to the doctor --"

The officer interrupted Martin's boring litany with a brusque wave of his hand for us to depart. If Martin had continued, I might have been given sainthood.

As we pulled away, I heard uneasy chuckles.

Pierre twittered, "They could lock us up forever, and no one would know."

"My office would know."

Nevertheless, I worried. If I had this kind of issue at the nonchalant, cigarette-hanging-from-lip checkpoint, what would occur in four hours at the fierce Hinche outpost?

Fording rivers and streams

Reaching the steeper mountains, I inserted a tape of Pavarotti arias. "We need opera to get over the mountains."

I began to sing dramatically along with the aria, "Nessun Dorma."

The surprised boys giggled and a few attempted to join in. Soon we all were singing, "Nessun Dorma. Nessun Dorma," or rather "Me san door may, door may, door me --"

We sang off-key, searching for rhythm and melody amid bursts of laughter. In comfortable silence, we descended. As we began to climb another mountain, I lifted my arm to indicate full choral volume.

During the trip, the boys uttered copious commands. When I wasn't going fast enough, they admonished me with "Ale, ale, ale" (go, go, go), impatiently motioning forward. When trailing a rickety *kamyonet* (large bob-truck) on an uphill, winding road, one shouted, "Take him now!" Never-ending hair pin turns were not considered.

While backing up at a rest stop, I looked over my shoulder to see through the rear window. I saw only craned, bobbing heads. Stretching their necks like roosters, they each crowed orders for my turns. Martin even grabbed the wheel to participate in the reverse direction.

"Stop! Everyone sit down so I can see."

Approaching the Hinche checkpoint, I breathed deeply and prayed for calm. The burly lieutenant, in his forties, sauntered to the car. His holster and pistol wobbled against his powerful thighs.

The lieutenant looked into the machine and surveyed the boys. Leaning on the windowsill, inches from my face, he asked the same questions as the Mirebelais commander.

"Where are you going?"

"To Le Jeune Mission."

"Who are you?"

Handing him my business card, I answered, "Madame Charlotte Wright."

He studied the card. "Who are these boys?"

"They're *timoun nan lari-yo* from Petionville. They're going to stay in the dormitory at Le Jeune. They've never seen this part of their country."

He said nothing.

I continued, "I did not want to drive alone. This was a good opportunity of showing them how beautiful the Plateau is."

My mouth was dry, but I tried to smile.

The lieutenant glanced over his shoulder toward his captain, who stood under a lone tree.

The captain nodded methodically.

The lieutenant opened the door and said, "Get out. Everyone get out."

The lieutenant and the captain searched the vehicle thoroughly. They lifted my suitcase, looked through my box of food and searched under the cargo carpet.

At that point, I wasn't too concerned. They would not find guns or drugs. However, my attitude changed when the lieutenant ordered me to a wooden platform attached to the small station.

Addressing the boys who had remained as still as statues, I said, "Get back in the car." When they hesitated, I repeated quietly and firmly, "Get in the machine."

The frightened boys barely moved as they climbed in, rolled up windows and locked doors.

The lieutenant pointed to a wooden table with two chairs on the platform. "Sit down."

I walked to the square table and observed a *rigoise* laid upon it. (a long, woven whip)

I chose the chair facing my vehicle, my back to the wall.

The lieutenant walked over to converse with his captain. By his thick belt, he pulled up his khaki pants over his hefty bulk, and in slow, deliberate steps, he approached the table and sat across from me.

His tongue cleaned his teeth behind his turgid lips as he stared.

Intimidation. The power strutting and measured movements were intentional, designed to intimidate me, and it was working.

I sent silent prayers upward for help.

The lieutenant picked up the whip. He slapped the leather handle in his palm and waited.

Slap, slap. Slap.

My eyes ran the length of the long whip and understood why the *rigoise* was called a cow's tail. Like a cat-o'-nine-tails but longer, leather strands had been woven together in the handle. When flayed, the victim suffered multiple wounds with one lash.

The lieutenant missed my shudder. He was looking toward the captain who remained within easy glance of the lieutenant and in my peripheral vision.

Removing his pistol, the lieutenant placed it with exaggerated movements next to the *rigoise*.

Silence pressed upon us.

This is a mind game. They want to frighten me, but probably don't know what to do with me. Stay calm, Charlotte. Stay calm.

Resisting the urge to speak first, I endured the oppressive silence. Discreetly, I wiped my sweating palms on my jeans and tightly clasped my hands in my lap. I wondered how much time needed to elapse before my staff initiated a search. I prayed again.

I stared at the yellow dust on my shoes, my dirt-caked socks, the gravel road, the cracked boards of the platform, the boys in the machine.

Adrien pressed his face against the glass, and even from my distance, I recognized his fear. I smiled weakly.

I looked at the thinning canopy of the lone, thirsty tree. I looked at anything but the whip and the gun.

Time ticked. I heard myself swallow.

The captain gave a methodic nod.

Inwardly, I braced myself. *Si Bon Dye vle.*

Like a stalking tiger, the lieutenant crouched across the table, and in English, demanded, "Where—is—your—father?"

What a most odd question.

"My father is in California."

His eyes widened and he leaned back, as though surprised. He mutely examined my passport for the umpteenth time.

"California?"

"Yes." As though presenting a tiresome school report, I

monotoned, "California is a state in the western part of the United States. My father lives there with my mother."

Tick-tock.

My father? Later I learned from the Round Table he was referring to Father Aristide who was a priest before he became President. Haitians and their metaphors. Where was my father? Where were my loyalties?

"What kind of work do you do?" he asked, reading my business card.

I recited the large development programs on the Central Plateau, the mother-child health, agriculture, reading.

He picked up my Washington State driver's license, and I trembled he would insist upon a Haitian one.

I spoke more animatedly. "We inoculate babies. We teach mothers how to prevent oral dehydration. We help farmers plant crops."

He still studied my driver's license.

Speaking more conversationally, I continued, reaching deep for minutia about the poor not having any tools for their crops. "The farmers need hoes and rakes. Without tools, the weeds take over the crops."

He looked up.

Finally, he'll say something.

He said nothing.

Our eye connection held for a few seconds while we took each other's measure.

This is a good man, trying to do his job and provide for his family.

The lieutenant shrugged toward the captain as if to say, "this woman is harmless." He returned my documents and escorted me to the vehicle.

After I got in, he leaned on the windowsill. With his back to the captain, he grinned broadly. When I started the machine, he looked at the boys, then at me and slapped the windowsill in friendly farewell.

He stopped short of sounding the deep, rich Caribbean laugh cavorting in his belly. But I heard it.

CHAPTER FIFTEEN

"Where love sets the table, the food tastes better."

— FRENCH PROVERB

Without a bright moon or city lights, even the tiniest of stars shone brilliantly against the midnight blue backdrop. The boys stared in awe. We sat on a small hill, counting and pointing.

"We don't see these stars in Port-au-Prince," said Nicolas.

"There's the Big Dipper," I said, helping them locate it.

"What's that whole section of stars?"

"The Milky Way."

"It looks like milk," said Adrien. He stretched his hand and traced the lavish road laced with millions of lights.

"There are stars from one edge of the sky clear to the other side," said Pierre. "I've never seen so many."

We sat in silence, some lying down on the hillside.

"I wanted to be a teacher," said Lucas.

"I wanted to be a teacher, too. You should be a singer," chimed Adrien. "Lucas can sing."

Lucas continued. "I lived in an orphanage because I wanted to learn to read. Then the *coup* happened. The French lady got scared and left, and the orphanage closed."

Cocooned in our reflections of dreams lost, we sat silently, lost in the universe, lost in ourselves, but together.

Pulling a long weed, I chewed on it, remembering my "what-might-have-been's and what-if's."

What happened?

I made other choices or met other needs, I suppose. I failed to honor my heart's desires. For these boys, external circumstances defined their possibilities. Yet, we each felt the residues of longing scattered in the corners of our hearts.

CHAPTER 15 | 179

On the hillside

Retiring from our reverie, the boys went to the dormitory, and I went to the main house. Since Tom and Mary had left Haiti, the housekeeper, Arelia, and others watched over us.

In the morning, I walked across the field to the cafeteria, anxious to hear how the boys enjoyed their night.

Arelia, a statuesque woman, black as the three caldrons beside her, greeted me in the cafeteria kitchen.

"They are so excited!" Her honeysuckle voice matched her eyes of joy. "*Bon Dye*, I loved their faces when I showed them how to use the showers, and I gave them soap. And to sleep on a bed!"

I smiled. "What time is--"

"Now stir that a little more. Add some salt," she said, pointing to a caldron managed by a young girl, a new cook. Turning to me, she said, "Bring the boys over in fifteen minutes."

We sat on benches at a long wooden table. In the center, Arelia placed a steaming bowl of soup and plates of bread.

The boys nudged each other, correcting their manners.

"Sit up straight, Pierre," said Martin.

"Use your spoon for the soup," Lucas said to Nicolas.

Adrien gently elbowed Rafel in the ribs. "Not now. Wait for the prayer."

Rafel dropped a knife heaped with butter, but held on to his bread.

They looked at each other.

"Who says the prayer?" Martin was impatient.

I uttered a prayer of gratitude. "Lord, thank you for your protection. Thank you for this wonderful food. Thank you for these boys and bless each one of them. In Christ's name, Amen."

"Rafel, you have to pour juice for others, not just yourself," whispered Lucas.

My heart expanded, and I breathed deeply to suppress tears. Their tender souls encased in their scrawny, toughened bodies needed so much nourishing. My love for them was like a passing shower upon parched earth.

"Sing, Lucas, sing," said Nicolas.

"What should I sing?"

"The Orphan's Song. Sing the Orphan's Song for Madame Charlotte."

Everyone quieted.

Lucas pursed his lips, rocking in rhythm to establish a beat. "*Jesu, Jesu, m'ginyan yon pwoblem.* (Jesus, Jesus, I've got a problem.) Got no mother. Got no father. I've got a problem."

"Sing it again, Lucas, please, more slowly so I can understand the words," I asked.

His crystal voice was surely a prayer to God. Everyone hushed, and Arelia stood in the rear, wiping her eyes with her apron. When Lucas came to the repetition of "got no mother, got no father," his voice broke, tears streamed, and he put his face down in his arms.

Adrien put his arm around him, and Pierre said, "You're making us all cry, even Madame Charlotte."

The teasing began again.

Dropping the boys at the Saturday marketplace, I gave each an allowance.

"You cannot bother me today," I said. "This is an important meeting. I'll pick you up at three this afternoon. Or you can return and wait in front for me."

Predictably, Martin had decided to join the boys at Le Jeune and not continue immediately to Cap-Haitien. Predictably, the only one who disturbed me at the office was my little whiner, Pierre.

Irritated, I walked to the gate when a staff member called me from the meeting, saying a boy was asking for me.

"What do you want?" I snapped. "I told you not to bother me."

Big tears formed in big eyes.

"I know, I know, Madame Charlotte. But Rafel asked me to share some of my money with him, and I did, but then he didn't keep his promise to share. It's not fair!"

"Aagh! Pierre, what am I going to do with you?"

"It's not fair!" he persisted.

Faced with the dilemma of Pierre's having a spoiled day and my worry about him or quickly giving in and returning to my meeting, I chose the latter.

Giving in is always the easy choice. As a mother, I claimed it bred leadership.

As we left Le Jeune, the excitement of their experiences in the dormitory and marketplace continued in the telling and re-telling of stories. No story ever becomes stale.

A quiet anxiety heightened as we approached the Hinche military checkpoint.

The burly lieutenant stepped to the middle of the road and held up his hand to halt. The stoic captain still stood under the solitary tree.

I rolled down the window.

The lieutenant ambled to the car and, as usual, stuck his head through to view the rear.

"Go on," he said, and smiling broadly, he waved us through.

As I drove away, I glanced in the rear-view mirror; he was still standing there, waving.

As we climbed the first mountain range, I said, "This calls for opera. We need opera to get us over the mountains."

Inserting a cassette, we sang along in our unique, personalized versions of Italian, belting out the high notes, then laughing.

"Nessun dorma," I belted.

"Me san door me," they mimicked.

From opera, we moved to hymns.

"Precious Lord, take my hand…"

I cleared my throat.

Help me, Lord, I prayed. *How do I tell them about the plot awaiting them in a few days?*

"Do you remember Izmery's funeral?" I asked.

They did.

"Two friends were outside the cathedral and overheard several *attachés* talking about the anniversary of the *coup* of President Aristide.

"Yes, yes," said Adrien with excitement. "September 30th is the anniversary. When is Titid coming back?"

Titid, the affectionate nickname the poor had bestowed upon Aristide.

"In a few weeks," said Nicolas.

Not likely, I thought. I watched them in the rear-view mirror.

"I heard some terrible rumors. You must listen and tell me if these can be true."

Hearing the gravity of my tone, they became still.

"Some friends said the *attachés* plan to kill the street boys in Petionville on the September 29th or 30th in celebration of the *coup*."

Rafel bit the inside of his lip, cocked his head and said, "It may be true. There are more beatings with whips, and last Friday night, they shot a boy."

"One of ours?"

"No," said Pierre. "The boy and Samuel were sitting on a tire. The *attaché* shot at Samuel, too, but he got away."

Target practice. Anger swelled within me. Not at the boys, but at a world in which youths assume getting shot at is part of normal life, like being involved in dangerous street fights or being always hungry.

I checked the rear-view mirror. They looked down or out the window.

Are they in denial? Maybe, since it's not the present moment, they can't comprehend it. I wondered if always living in the present moment blocked memories of the past and fear of the future?

"How old was he?" I asked.

"About ten," said Adrien.

"Why isn't this known? What about the U.N. monitors?"

No one answered.

Finally, Lucas said, "They take the body away."

"It wouldn't matter anyway," muttered Rafel.

The truth of that statement slapped my face.

Wake up, Charlotte. Who can they turn to for help? There's no justice system, no police to aid them, no school or institution.

Silence lay heavy for the next mile.

These boys weren't in denial. They understood their reality far better than I. They feared hunger and injury, violence and death, but they were powerless. They dealt with fear by laughter or silence.

That's the Haitian way. Silence. If they remained quiet, they might survive.

"Do you believe this plan for attacking the street boys can happen?" I asked.

"Yes," said several simultaneously.

"Please. You must leave the city and return to the provinces."

No one spoke. In the mirror, I saw they were perplexed, exchanging glances and elbows.

Pierre lost the elbow nomination. "We have no money to go the provinces, Madame Charlotte, and even if we did, many of us have no province to go to. We have no family, and no one to beg from."

Of course.

"At least get off the streets. Can you get off the streets?"

They huddled, and I heard twitters of whispered conversation.

Adrien said, "Pierre and Lucas can stay with me at my mother's place in the ravine. We'll tell the little ones who have a family, like the twins, to stay at home."

"We can sleep in smaller groups and hide at night," said Nicolas.

"But Madame Charlotte, we need to beg during the day. We have to eat," said Pierre.

"We can stay in crowds," said Adrien.

"You have to keep a low profile," I said. "Stay in crowds, but not the obvious places like Lynx Air or the grocery store. Today is September 19th. For the next weeks you absolutely must disappear as much as possible. Is that clear? Promise me!"

They promised.

"*Ale, ale, ale.*"

CHAPTER SIXTEEN

"You are not a fish. You were not intended for the net."

— *HAITIAN PROVERB*

I smiled at the bouquet of summer daisies and coral asters. *Possibly taken from a cemetery. From the deceased to the living on today, September 27th, my birthday.*

"How old are you, Madame?" asked little Boniface, who had joined the ensemble.

"Old enough to be a *grunmoun*. When's your birthday?"

"I don't know," he said, looking downcast.

"A lot of us don't know our birthdays, Madame."

My birthday, September 27th

"I'll tell you what," I said, tilting his chin toward me, "I'll give you mine."

His eyes brightened. "Really?"

"Really. I'm not counting mine anymore. From now on, September 27th is your birthday."

During the night of September 28th, the paramilitary gathered in the ravine for a real hurrah. Drums pounded for Ogoun, god of War. Chanting escalated with spontaneous shouting, pistol shots, and obviously growing numbers.

"Again?" said Shelley, parting the mosquito net and climbing into my bed.

A monotone horn droned its haunting, single wavelength in minor key, transmitting its call for Ogoun in the spirit world. Shelley covered her ears.

"This is ridiculous! Every night! Get a life!" She slapped and arranged a pillow. "Why are they doing this?"

"They're angry. They're calling down their god of War against the Americans. Everyone knows the military leaders are breaking the Accords. Aristide is not coming back. They are not going away. They have a lot to lose if the Americans invade." I stroked her hair. "And the anniversary of the *coup* is part of it."

"Well, we're losing sleep! What will they lose?"

"Power."

I listened to the paramilitary *attachés* chanting in unison. *Would they hurt the street boys?*

By five o'clock, inebriation and fatigue won out, and the sonorous chanting transmuted to sluggish, random calling.

On September 29, 1993, as usual, I parked in front of Presse Evangelique. I opened the car door to face eight terrified boys racing toward me.

"They are chasing us!"

Charles lifted his shirt. A band of red welts wrapped his ribcage. "An *attaché* beat me with his baton last night, but I got away."

A boy screamed, and I looked up the street. Two *attachés* stalked the boys. One rhythmically cracked a fifteen-foot whip, a *rigoise*, like a cowboy herding cattle.

At each whistling crack, the street boys screamed and ran faster toward us.

Numb, I stood still.

As the children neared, the *attachés* saw me standing by my open car door. They slowed and stood nearby.

I wanted to puke. *It's really happening.*

Samuel reached into my machine and retrieved my briefcase. He wore a fine pair of sunglasses with metal frames, highly treasured and undoubtedly filched.

I walked to the open gate and waited.

A tall *attaché* charged over to Samuel, pointed to my briefcase, and shouting in heated, rapid Creole, ordered him to put down my briefcase.

Defiant, wearing his sunglasses with stars, Samuel smarted off, an offense tantamount to a finger gesture.

CHAPTER 16 | 193

I put up my hand to intervene, but the *attaché* exploded and rapidly pulled a nine-millimeter gun from under his shirt.

Samuel dropped the briefcase with a thud and started running toward the gate. Other boys screamed and fled to the other side of the street.

Chasing him, the *attaché* targeted his gun toward Samuel's back. But Samuel reached the gate, flew by me and dodged around a bush on the grounds.

A metallic taste swabbed my throat.

The attacker raced through the gate after Samuel. I felt the body heat of his rage like a passing wind, and I saw in his liquid eyes that he had gone mad.

I gripped my stomach, immobile, not believing what was happening.

The *attaché* had charged ten feet into the private grounds of Presse Evangelique when he saw that employees had come to the front door. He stopped and searched the sky in a circular motion, as though he had lost his sense of direction. Then he whirled and stormed back toward me.

As the *attaché* retreated, his gun inadvertently swung at me. I saw the barrel, and I felt the solid, heavy weight of the cylinder. Pure fear seized me. The power in a trigger pull. A click. A piercing bullet. A life gone.

Then he charged past me to the middle of the street toward the boys who were hiding behind my machine. Scattering in panic, screaming, they ran through the iron gate.

More street boys came running down the street, and still more. A stampeding migration of fear, they fled through the iron gates of refuge.

The *attaché* turned in circles, perhaps searching for someone, perhaps confused about what to do.

I dashed through the iron gate.

From among the employees, Baptiste hurried out.

As I was muttering "Baptiste, it's really happening. They're going to kill them," he closed the gates.

Saying nothing, we looked at one another.

My entire body quivered. *Stay calm. Breathe, breathe.*

I looked at the boys who gathered in small groups. The words of the Embassy official returned. I could tell them to hide, to go to the provinces and walk away.

That's the sane solution. But it's not the right solution. It's not God's solution.

I took out a pad and pen from my briefcase, which Samuel had dropped near me and which I had retrieved. "Line up. Give me your name, your original province and tell me if you have someone there to take care of you."

The boys quickly lined up. *Thank you, God, for the clothing exercise.*

The first in line said, "Philippe."

My hand visibly shook as I scrawled his name.

What am I doing? What about Shelley?

"Go over there, by the tree. Next."

"Etienne."

What will happen to Shelley?

My nose burned and my eyes watered. I tried to write "Etienne," and I missed the paper line completely.

"Here, let me," said Baptiste, taking the pad and pen from me.

I stood beside him as each boy took his orderly turn.

Waiting on the other side of the iron fence, three *attachés* glared, one with a gun and two carrying long whips.

A fourth *attaché* arrived, and I shuddered when I saw him. Wearing a peach linen shirt and gold necklaces, the leader clung to the gate with his fists. For a moment, I thought he might climb it.

My stomach rolled, and a metallic taste returned to paint my mouth.

What am I doing? I should tell the boys to run and hide, and I should go inside and wash my hands of this Haitian mess.

"What are we going to do, Madame Charlotte?"

I looked into the trusting eyes of young, scrawny Garry Jean. I fought tears.

Yes, Lord, what are we going to do? There's no going back. I've passed the point of no return. God help me. Show me what to do. Protect my daughter.

"Go sit in a circle over there." I motioned to a grassy area among birds of paradise on the side of the building.

"What are you going to do?" asked Baptiste.

"Get them out of the city."

"Wait here for a while. The *attachés* will tire of waiting. They'll leave."

I called the boys to sit down among the birds of paradise and stood before them. "Do you remember how we did the clothing at the office? When we went down in three groups?"

They nodded. No one said a word.

I took a deep breath. *Stay calm. Stay ordered.*

"We're going to do that again. You stay on this far side of the building and be quiet. At eleven, I'll come back for the little ones. We'll go to my office. You'll get an envelope with money for a one-way bus ticket to your province and a meal. My driver will take you to the bus in *la ville*.

"At twelve, I'll return for the middle group, and finally, I'll be back at one o'clock for the oldest boys."

They sat unmoving. No questions, no elbows or jostling or jumping up.

The tightness in my chest loosened. Indecision vanished. I had made an irrevocable choice. I would do what God put upon my heart and what was before me. I would rescue these boys and trust that God would protect both my daughter and me.

"Do you understand?"

Henri spoke up. "Yes, three groups, just like before. What about the boys who stay here and hide?"

"They'll get an envelope, too, so they won't have to beg for a while."

"How long do we have to stay away?"

"Until it's safe to return."

"You mean until Titid comes back in October?" asked Adrien.

Convinced by the Round Table, I knew Aristide would not return in October.

"Try for Christmas."

"Move to the back of the building," Baptiste ordered the boys. Turning to me, he said, "When the *attachés* can't see them or us, they'll leave. Let's go inside and wait."

He was right, as he always was. The *attachés* left, and I left for the office. Using petty cash money, my staff assembled envelopes, each with the boy's name and province.

When I arrived at eleven, pandemonium erupted. The youngest group was climbing into the rear when suddenly, Lucas grabbed my arm and pointed down the street.

"*Attachés!*"

The boys screamed, shoved, and pushed to get into the

machine. I grabbed two older boys by the shirttails and pulled them out.

"There's no room," I said. "The youngest group only. The rest run and hide. I'll be back at noon."

Baptiste climbed into the passenger seat.

"What are you doing?" I asked.

"I'm going with you."

"No, Baptiste."

The *attachés* were now trotting toward us.

I started the engine and turned around.

"Get out now, Baptiste. You're putting your life in danger."

"So are you, Charlotte. Let's go."

At the office, it was clockwork. Envelopes, kisses and into the jeep the boys climbed, and my worker drove them away.

"That went well," I said as Baptiste and I returned to Petionville.

"Let's hope the next group does the same."

I drove up the hill on the one-way avenue and slowed for the turn that led to Presse Evangelique.

"Stop!" Baptiste said.

Adrien and Pierre jumped from behind bushes, frantically waving their arms. Other boys streamed from bushes and over walls.

"The *attachés*," they panted; "they're waiting for you!"

I pulled over, staring blankly at more boys who came running through the streets to reach the machine.

Ahead two *attachés* strode toward us, a tall one with a whip and a short one with a gun.

"Baptiste, will they shoot?"

"Not here, not now, not in broad daylight on a busy street. At least, I don't think so."

The machine rocked as the panicked boys fought their way into the rear.

The two *attachés* approached my window.

"We're stuck," I mumbled to Baptiste. "No way out of this. Be ready for some quick translations."

He nodded.

"Where are you going?" asked the one with the whip.

I tightened my knuckles around the steering wheel.

"What's the problem?" I asked.

The short one fingered his thick moustache. His gun see-sawed in his hand as though it were too heavy for his thin wrist. The tall one stared at me while he methodically rolled his whip.

"The boys are garbage," said the one with the gun. "They need to be thrown away."

Vermin, children without mamas. I've heard that before. Stay calm.

"Jesus loves these children, just as Jesus loves you," I said. "Do you think Jesus loves you?"

"*Oui*, Jesus loves me," the gunman said. "What's your name?"

"Madame Charlotte."

"Where do you live?"

Baptiste quickly interjected "Petionville" and shot me a glance that said "give nothing more."

"Where are you going with the *timoun nan lari-yo*?" the whip man asked.

I spoke slowly and deliberately, motioning for Baptiste to translate. "I'm giving them a little trip. Someone needs to care for these children. Isn't it sad these children don't have a mother or father to love and care for them?"

The man with the gun paused, mouth half open, as though that were a novel thought. His eyes wandered.

He's high on drugs or still hung over from the Vodou ceremony last night.

"How many children do you have, Messieur?" I asked.

"Seven."

"How many do you have?" I asked the one with the whip.

"Three."

"I know you love your children very much."

"Oh, yes," the whip man said. "I pay one hundred and fifty dollars each month for my sons to attend school."

"And you?" I asked the gunman. "Do your children go to school?"

"All of them," he said proudly.

At that moment, Haiti's tragedy seemed so clear. Who's going to eat? Who's going to send their children to school? The group in power. Death to those who try to take that away. Aristide's return would flip the balance of power.

I leaned over the window. "Isn't it sad these boys don't have a good father like you?"

The gunman thought for a moment, waving his unstable nine-millimeter in the air. "Yes. I don't know why they run from me."

Definitely under the influence.

"If I saw your gun and your whip, I'd run, too."

Baptiste nudged my arm and nodded up the street.

The leader in the costly peach linen shirt and gold jewelry bore down upon us.

Shifting into gear, I said "Time to go" and floored the accelerator.

The shocked leader attempted to flag me down. As I sped past him, his face contorted in fury.

Since I was forced to drive up the hill and circle the block to reach the descending one-way avenue, I knew the leader on foot could cut us off. I held the steering wheel tightly and pressed the accelerator, taking the corners as fast as I dared.

Forever in the present moment, some of the boys squealed in delight.

"He'll get us in the marketplace," whispered Baptiste.

When I reached the parallel avenue and began the descent, I accelerated again. In the rearview mirror, I saw him.

"He's behind us. Running hard."

"The market's ahead," said Baptiste. "You'll have to slow down."

The Petionville marketplace loomed with its hundreds of pedestrians. I slowed as the crowd blocked the narrow street.

"He's gaining on us."

Baptiste looked over his shoulder and wiped sweat from his forehead.

I looked at the pedestrian congestion. Heart thumping, I prayed, "Dear God, let this market open like the Red Sea."

I laid on the horn.

The leader was now only a few yards back. I swallowed hard.

After two quick blasts and a long one, the crowd parted. The path completely cleared, and I accelerated. As I passed, people flowed again behind us, closing off my view of the peach linen shirt.

CHAPTER SEVENTEEN

"If God sends you, He pays your expenses."

— *HAITIAN PROVERB*

Sitting in a circle, the boys received their envelopes and dawdled by the jeep that would take them to the bus.

A question echoed through the group. "Madame Charlotte, will you be here when we get back?"

I nodded. At least I hoped I would be.

I hugged each one and kissed their cheeks.

Without his sunglasses, Samuel sat crying on the ground.

"Why is Samuel crying?" I asked.

Pierre leaned down to him, and when they had finished whispering, he leaned to my ear and said, "Because Madame Charlotte did not kiss his cheek."

Bending over, I took his face in my hands and kissed his cheek. *They are so hungry for a mother's touch.*

"Are you really going back?" asked Baptiste as he climbed into the jeep with the driver to the bus station. "You shouldn't, you know."

"I gave my word. I'll take another route. Henri can walk those big boys to the office. You take care of yourself, my friend."

Shelley dropped her backpack on the tile floor and stood in shock.

"You did WHAT?"

"Pack a bag. Take your books and your tennis racket."

"Will we evacuate?"

Aching, I heard her desperation. I walked over and hugged her. "We'll stay at the Villa and you'll still go to school. We'll get good advice and decide what to do. We're not going to panic. Now pack your bag."

Shelley walked in a circle, still holding her head. Oh,

Mother!" she wailed. "How could you do this to me? To us?"

A wave of remorse swept over me. Perhaps I made the wrong decision. All I could say was "I didn't have a choice."

"You tell me we always have choices, Mom."

Her shoulders slumped. My guilt increased.

"I didn't have time to think, Shelley. Everything happened so fast."

She sank into a chair and put her face in both hands.

I went to her, bent on my knees, and put my arms around her. Tears flowed down my cheeks, and rocking, I squeezed her tighter. "Shelley, I love you."

She remained silent.

"Maybe you're right. I did have a choice, but I couldn't turn the other way, Shelley! I just couldn't do it! These boys have no one. They starve; they get injured! Now people want to kill them just for surviving!"

I started crying. "I believe God will protect us."

Shelley didn't move.

"You'll still go to school, so pack your things. Go on now."

I pulled her to her feet.

"For how long?"

"For a few days, maybe a week. If necessary, we'll go to Miami until it's safe. We'll be all right. Go on now."

When she came out of her room with her bags, I asked, "Where's your tennis racket?"

Shelley returned with her racket and swished it once. "Maybe it won't be so bad," she said without belief. "My friends can visit every afternoon. We can play tennis and have Pina Coladas."

"Virgin."

When we checked into the Hotel Villa, I related a quick summary of why we were there. The clerk put us on the third floor adjacent to a Colonel with the Royal Canadian Mounted Police.

In the Villa lounge, I related the incident to my friend, the ophthalmologist, and his friend from the Venezuelan Embassy.

The Venezuelan diplomat insisted I meet the Venezuelan Ambassador and tell her what occurred. He scurried across the dining room to locate her.

Tall, with red hair and intelligent eyes, Elsa graciously

listened. "You must speak to the representatives of your country," she said.

I was processing this when she added, "for your own protection. The U.S. Colonel of Special Forces is having dinner over there." She pointed to a table of four men. "Do you plan to stay in the hotel?"

"For a few days. I don't know what to do."

"Stay here for a week. Let the situation calm down. The *attachés* will get over this plan and move on to another one. That's Haiti."

"A week?"

"That should do it."

Elsa knew Haiti well and as the Ambassador from Venezuela, she had been involved with President Aristide's evacuation after the *coup*. In fact, it had been Venezuela that took him out of the country. I trusted her advice.

As I walked toward the Colonel's table, self-doubt assailed me. I glanced over my shoulder and saw Elsa watching.

Perhaps I'm making too much of this, I thought. *I don't want to disturb anyone's dinner, particularly the Colonel's. I already disturbed him with my illness on the first day of his arrival.*

Standing beside him, I cleared my throat. He looked up.

"The Venezuelan Ambassador suggested I speak with you about an incident today. I'm an American, Charlotte--"

He put down his fork. "Yes, I remember you. You're looking much better." He smiled and looked over at Elsa.

I saw her give him a slight nod.

"Sit down," he said, pulling up a chair. "What's going on?"

I tried to be as succinct as possible. His chicken was getting cold.

"Sergeant," he called to an adjacent table.

The sergeant came to his side. I recognized him as one who often sat with the medic.

"Call the Montana Hotel and ask the Canadians to send down several armed guards for the night. Post them around the hotel."

As an aside to me, he said, "The U.S. Congress did not allow our Forces to bring guns, but the Canadians have them."

I couldn't digest that non-sequitur.

"Then take this lady to the operations room and get a statement."

Room 101 was an oversized guest room occupied by the sergeant and used as a central storage and meeting area for the advance logistics group of Special Forces.

Sergeant Bell pulled up a Louis XIV chair for me and placed it beside the king-sized bed where he sat with pen and paper in hand.

"Go," he said, motioning for me to sit. "From the beginning."

When I said I had returned to Petionville for the third group, he put the pen down and shook his head.

"You went back? Again? A third time?"

He thinks I'm out of my mind.

"Look," I said, swinging my crossed leg in agitation, "I told them I would come back, and I did. I just took another route."

The sergeant's eyes lingered on my leg.

I looked down. My buttoned red skirt had fallen slightly open. I uncrossed my legs and straightened my skirt to cover my knees.

"What should I do?"

He looked up abruptly.

"You've embarrassed their leader, the guy in the peach shirt. Have a friend drive your daughter to and from school. Switch vehicles. Drive one they won't recognize as yours. Tell your daughter what's happening. Tell her not to worry, just to be aware of who and what is happening around her. That's good advice for you, too."

Our eyes met only for a moment.

CHAPTER EIGHTEEN

"A woman is like mahogany. The older she is, the better."

— HAITIAN PROVERB

The next day when I descended the marble stairs, Sergeant Bell rose from his chair in the dining area. Short, stocky, and blue-eyed, he strode toward me.

A man of grit.

"How's your day?"

"Good--"

"Here, let's sit for a minute." He pulled out a chair for me.

Sergeant Bell was all business with brusque, efficient movement.

"Did you switch vehicles?"

"Yes, this morning. I'm now driving a beaten-up jeep."

"Good. And Shelley?"

"A friend took her to school, and she'll return with her other friends. They'll do homework or play tennis or swim. She's okay."

"What's your routine?"

I welcomed his interest like an unexpected breeze. I felt like someone actually cared.

"What about Shelley? How's she doing?"

"She's okay. Shelley adapts well."

"How does she do in school?"

"She's a good student. Tomorrow night is her Open House; I'll learn more then."

"What time is that?"

"Seven."

He studied me. "You should not be going out at night alone."

"Uh--well, I'm not going to miss it."

"I'll make arrangements and go with you."

"That's not necessary--"

"It is necessary."

One of his men hailed him.

He slapped the table. "Gotta go. Catch you later."

"Sergeant Bell, did the Canadians come last night?"

"They came. Several vehicles drove in and fired shots, circled and left. They didn't return."

He turned to leave, then stopped. "Don't be so formal. Call me Craig or Bell." He grinned.

When we greeted each other the following day, he said, "Remember to wait for me tonight to go to the Open House."

Later, after work and seated in the lounge, he watched Shelley swimming in the nearby pool.

"Shelley's a good swimmer. It's important her life remain as normal as possible right now."

Our chit-chat floated above a chemistry of undercurrents. For the first time in seven years, I didn't feel completely alone.

Preparing for the Open House, I applied finishing touches to my make-up and turned sideways to check my figure in the mirror. *A little tummy, but slim.* At 6:30 I walked to the dining area.

Sergeant Bell was not dressed for an Open House. In the lounge, he sat in his shorts and tank top, engaged in conversation with several of his men.

I stood near the marble stairs, uncertain of what to do. I checked the time. I wondered if I should interrupt him, ask if he has time to go.

Indecision led to simply waiting by the stairs. Tick-tock. Tick-tock. At 6:45, I left.

When I returned several hours later, Shelley and her friend had finished homework and were waiting in the lobby for her friend's father.

"I'm joining the Round Table on the balcony," I said. "Come out there when you're ready."

In a private alcove off the lounge, a half-moon balcony hung suspended over a lush garden. The makeup of the Round Table on that evening had changed.

Our rum-drinking, animated Paul was missing. However, several others had joined the group, which sat in a formal semi-circle. Shelley came behind me, and we took the last two wrought iron chairs adjacent to the lounge.

Under the hum of the group's orderly conversation, Shelley asked, "How was the Open House?"

"Terrific! You're doing really well. Your science teacher says you have a gift."

She raised her eyebrows.

"A gift," I repeated.

Shelley leaned down and took a handful of peanuts from the glass coffee table. "Cool," she said, munching away. "Sergeant Bell is upset with you."

"Why?"

"He told you to wait for him, and you didn't. He was mad, Mom."

Over Shelley's shoulder, I glanced toward the restaurant area. At that moment, Craig strode by, still in shorts and tank top. He stared our way without smiling or pausing.

Annoyed, my ribcage tightened.

"Well, he was late. No big deal."

At 10:00, Craig re-appeared, scrubbed and changed. He

looked over the tight little group, leaving momentarily to return with a chair.

I blinked in amazement as he edged the chair into the group, forcing everyone to scoot in order to make room for him. Then, there he was, sitting across from me in dress slacks and shirt with top button open.

Awkward surprise hung over the half-moon balcony. Behaving like a barnyard full of chickens when a new rooster enters, the Round Table looked at him, at me, back to him, then at each other. They waited for introductions.

Shelley elbowed me out of shock.

"Um-this is Sergeant Bell. He's with the Special Forces. This is--" and I went around the circle giving names and what each did in Haiti. Some had to be introduced to me.

The group conversation reverted to an English garden 18th Century variety, all niceness and refined decorum. *Where are our tea and crumpets?* Funny how the absence of key people and the addition of new ones change the tenor of a group. I missed our humorous and informative Round Table conversation.

Sergeant Bell leaned over the coffee table. In harmony with the 18th Century garden tone, he politely said, "You didn't wait," but his eyes flashed reproach.

I politely responded, "I didn't have time."

"I told you to wait. That I was going with you." His words, spoken in irritation, jarred the garden hummingbird conversation. Several looked our way.

I cleared my throat. The hummingbirds began their exploration of flowers again.

Folding my arms, I leaned over and recited, "I did wait. You were with your men. You were busy. I had to leave."

His irritation was visible. "Any problems?"

"I went through a roadblock on the way back."

He grimaced. "What kind of roadblock?"

"Rolled barbed wire. Military. At least it wasn't paramilitary."

He looked toward the restaurant where a few of his men had gathered. "Why didn't you come and get me?"

"I didn't want to bother you," I said and casually examined a fingernail.

Craig leaned back and half-smiled. His eyes relaxed in a twinkle, and he interjected himself in the tea and crumpet conversation.

I smiled. Demurely, I think.

He's probably in his late thirties, too young for me.

Someone asked him what the Special Forces Logistics Team did. He explained they were to ensure preparations were made for the docking of the *USS Harlan County* ship that carried Marines, scheduled to arrive in mid-October, only two weeks away. The Marines would ensure the peaceful transfer of power from General Cedras and the military to the democratically elected President Aristide. At least, that was the agreement of the Accords.

I didn't share the opinion of the Round Table, simply put, that the Haitian stall would kick in, and it would never occur. Hence, their plans to close the factories and leave the country were well underway.

I had begun warming to the notion of overcoming my age difference objections with Craig until one of his men arrived and said, "There's a party in Sue's room. Are you coming?"

Sue was one of several young girls with CARE. I slammed the mental door on any romance, and it must have shown on my face. I gave my full attention to the garden conversation.

Craig looked perplexed. "Later," he said to his buddy.

Still, he remained until Shelley and I left.

I dreamed about Craig Bell that night, and upon awakening, the residue was a deep ache of loneliness. When Shelley went to the bathroom, I rolled into a ball with clenched fists and cried.

When Shelley returned, I wiped my eyes and hurried to the bathroom. Yet like water seeping through cracks in a dam, my tears lingered.

I brushed my hair slowly.

"You like him, don't you?"

I could only nod.

Shelley tossed her hands in the air. "What's the problem? Is he married?"

"No, divorced, but he's much too young."

"This is the 20th Century, Mother. Age doesn't matter."

"Shelley, he's probably forty at most. I'm fifty-two."

She answered my shrug with "so what."

I contemplated possibilities. *This would be a wartime romance. It can't last.*

"Hello, Mom. He likes you."

I finished placing a pin in my hair. "How do you know that?"

"Mom, wake up. He watches you."

"He does?"

"Yeah, like when you cross a room or laugh. Don't be dense. The man talks to me, Mom, ME. Why? Because he likes you. Last night he sat with those strangers -- " She started laughing. "Trust me, Mom, go for it."

"About ready?" I asked.

"Remember, a group's getting together tonight, and I'm spending the night at Marilyn's. You do remember, right?"

I nodded, and we coordinated pick-up.

"Mom, seriously, you need to liven up. Like--what happened to the unrealistic dreamer?"

I snorted, laughing to myself. *Romance advice from a fourteen-year-old.* More poignantly, I realized she wanted me to be happy.

I didn't see Craig until evening in the lounge.

"Where's Shelley?"

"At a friend's house."

"All night?"

CHAPTER 18 | 223

I tightened my hand around the Perrier bottle. Without looking at him, I said "yeah."

Leaning on the bar, Craig looked toward the pool and twirled his beer a time or two.

"Do you want to see a movie?"

My stomach flip-flopped.

Silence seemed to hover forever before I muttered, "Sounds good."

Craig tapped the bar with his fingers. The bartender turned to receive his order.

"No, I was just tapping--"

The bartender glanced at me and smiled. Like the street boys, my daughter, Arthur, and the Villa Creole employees, everyone rooted for me to find a companion. Hugo in Pignon said it. "In Haiti, no one is alone."

"Your room?" he asked and tilted his head.

Off-guard, my mouth paused on half-open. I hadn't considered where we would watch a borrowed hotel video. I rested my chin in my hand. "That may not be such a good idea," I hedged. With each word I could feel myself pushing away.

Flight. Again. No. No. No.

"The operations room has too many interruptions." He narrowed his brows and waited, but I looked away.

I knew I only had to say "not my room," and our relationship would remain at best platonic, and at worse, gasp its last breath.

I slowly smiled. "Sure."

Craig exhaled relief.

We checked out an action movie at the front desk, and awkwardly, talking in fragments, we went to my room on the third floor.

Sitting on the bed, he clicked the remote to start the film. Gradually, he eased over, and slipping his arm around me, gingerly nuzzled my neck. The last rampart, that lone parapet of emotional isolation, crumbled.

In the following days, a lightness came over me. Images of the street boys in my mind wandered like leaves carried by a gentle breeze. The magnitude of what they brought to my life became clear.

These boys who have great needs give great gifts. In caring for them, I found a part of me I thought lost.

CHAPTER NINETEEN

"If you are not a lion, make yourself a fox."

— HAITIAN PROVERB

As the Venezuelan Ambassador predicted, the paramilitary *attachés* forgot us, and Shelley and I returned home.

The countdown for the agreed upon time for Aristide's return was ticking. Tension mounted. The Round Table continued to state that the military would never step down, that their ploy of the stall would work.

The Special Forces' logistics team, including Craig, maintained that the military would step down. After all, the ship *USS Harlan County* carrying American Marines was on its way.

As the *USS Harlan County* ploughed through Caribbean waters toward Haiti, the volatility of the *Vodou* ceremonies in our ravine went ballistic. Literally.

Heated speeches over a loudspeaker with an amplifying system assaulted our little home every night. The vehemence in the male warrior's voice echoed fiery sermons, predicting defeat and death to American soldiers. They unleashed their fury in war chants and gunfire and cries of solidarity. Pounding drums for Ogoun, god of War, they worked themselves into a frenzy.

"Mom, I can't sleep!" Shelley shouted as she came into my room, fists closed in complete exasperation.

"Neither can I."

"Every night, every night," she wailed. "This used to happen only on weekends. Now it's every night with drums and chanting. And speeches over loudspeakers!"

She slugged a pillow several times.

I picked up my Bible.

The neighbors' generators clicked on.

"Wish we had one of those to drown them out," said Shelley.

"Me, too."

Without that luxury, we lay awake for hours listening to vitriolic speeches and a crescendo of drums.

Before the *USS Harlan County* could dock, the *attachés* held a general strike and swarmed the harbor area. To be convincing, the paramilitary kidnapped hundreds of *tap-tap's* (public taxis) and forced people to demonstrate against the arrival of the ship. They presented a "no one wants Americans here" protest.

At the Villa, everyone anxiously awaited the American response.

Craig thumped his fist as we stood at the end of a crowded bar after work.

"The President has ordered the ship not to land the Marines," he said quietly.

I rolled my eyes.

"Doesn't the government know that the paramilitary kidnapped all of those people?"

"They know. They don't want a repeat of the military tragedy that just happened in Somalia."

My stomach knotted.

"So, the bullies are going to win," I said. "Armed thugs kidnap and force the *tap-tap's* with its hundreds of passengers to demonstrate at the dock, and the Americans interpret it as everyone is against the Marines landing. Another Somalia in the making."

Craig slapped the bar counter. "That's about it."

The bartender turned to take his order, and Craig shook his head "no."

My irritation turned to pleading.

"You saw the television news. Only the *attachés* are waving guns. The others are innocent by-standers forced to stand by the dock. The American military will be welcomed here. You know that. The people want Titid to return!"

"It's no use, Charlotte. It's not up to me."

Musical strains of Enya, which I had come to associate with early Villa evenings, resonated over our silence.

Someone pushed to the bar behind me, and I moved closer to Craig.

"Remember when the Commander sat with you last week?"

"Hmmm-hum."

"He stayed so long that I imagined a news flash. 'Sergeant Kills Commander in Jealous Rage Over Missionary.'"

"I saw you pacing back and forth."

The music switched from Enya to Kenny G and the "Theme of Dying Young." The haunting saxophone heralded the loss I knew was coming.

"You'll be leaving soon. Won't you?"

"I don't know what we'll do," he said without looking at me. "The President can't make up his mind. First, they're going to land. Then they're not. The events in Somalia changed things here."

Everything and everyone are connected.

For the next two days, the *USS Harlan County* drifted on the seas between American indecision and paramilitary threats of violence.

Then the ship sailed away.

When I arrived to meet Craig for dinner and saw the unusual flurry of activity, I had a sudden intake of breath. Craig was giving orders to his men on the terrace. This was it. They were leaving.

He hurried toward me.

Taking my hand, he said, "We have twenty minutes to say good-bye. We pull out at dawn."

He walked me to my machine.

"We'll be back."

"When?"

"I don't know."

"If the government is waiting for the people to revolt, it won't happen. They'll just endure."

"Charlotte, take your daughter and leave. It's going to get rough."

"It's rough now."

"Nothing compared to what will happen here before we invade."

"The invasion will occur?"

"Yeah."

"When?"

He shrugged. "Anywhere from six months to a year."

"I'll stay. There's chatter that the airlines will announce a date when all flights stop. Round Table says that's the latest time to leave."

He shook his head.

"Craig, look at Shelley. She has friends. Good teachers, good school. She is flourishing. We'll be here until school closes. Probably June. We'll be careful."

The warmth of his breath upon my neck was a feather's caress.

The Americans may come, but you won't be back, I thought. *I'll never see you again.*

At four-thirty on the morning of October 16th, 1993, I lay in bed and heard the convoy descending John Brown Avenue. I walked to the balcony railing and listened to the only sound in the stillness, the rumbling of U.S. vehicles as they made their way to the airport.

With a broken spirit, I sobbed for my loss. I sobbed for the street boys, for our people on the Central Plateau where life would be insufferable. Dawn stretched its arms of pink above the mountains, and the early morning breeze cooled my tears.

I thought of David when he wrote Psalms during his despair. In my despair, I cried, *Please, God, help Haiti.*

One by one, the U.S. planes departed in the distance, and with them went the hopes of a nation.

CHAPTER TWENTY

"With patience, you will see the belly button of the ant."

— *HAITIAN PROVERB*

Arriving in two's or three's, the street boys returned to Petionville by Christmas.

"Madame Charlotte," they shouted. Henri picked me up and swung me in circles. Calling "Mama, Mama," Adrien raced down the hill, and Pierre hopped on his imaginary pogo stick. Samuel stood shyly by the curb until I went to him.

When we united with hugs in the street, the *marchands*

laughed heartily, holding their headscarves or tugging their aprons.

In December 1993, the goodwill lauded by the Christmas season held sway. More electricity, more music and concerts, less rattling of machine guns in the night.

A festive atmosphere pervaded the streets of Petionville. Traffic inched. Music played. Pedestrians laughed. Older street boys sold packages of Juicy Fruit gum from willow baskets.

All in the blessed light of full electricity. We had streetlights, strung lights, neon lights. The celebration honored a musician, Sweet Mickey, who was playing at the Garage, a nightclub across from the pizza cafe.

Shelley, now fifteen, and three friends came from the hamburger hangout when she saw me pull up in front. She asked to go to the Garage to hear Sweet Mickey.

"It's a nightclub, isn't it?"

"Everyone's going, Mom. Look around. There are hundreds of people on the street. When will it be like this again?"

True.

The Round Table speculated this night of joviality and electric light was a peace offering to the people for the military's refusal to cede power. The Accords were publicly finished.

"How 'bout this? I'll go to the pizza cafe across the street from the Garage, and I'll be on the patio in case you need me. I expect you by ten o'clock. How's that?"

The kids talked it over. "That gives us an hour and a half," said Marilyn. "Plenty of time."

"Do you want to ride?"

They looked at the traffic back-up and laughed.

A happy group of teenagers joined the mélange of pedestrians weaving between cars, headlights casting their animated shadows upon the vehicles behind them.

Led by Lucas, several street boys swam against the pedestrian streams until they reached me. Lucas's taciturn expression suggested a boy on a mission.

"Madame Charlotte," he said, trotting beside my machine as the traffic inched forward. "Madame Charlotte, Shelley is going into the Garage. Do you want me to stop her?"

If Shelley ever had privacy in this town, it's gone forever, I thought in amusement.

"No, it's okay. I'm waiting for her at the pizza cafe. She's to meet me at ten."

Lucas turned to the boys behind him, announcing, "Mademoiselle Shelley's okay. It's okay." His manner was like that of a father quieting troubled children. Still trotting beside my machine, he said, "I'll stand guard outside the Garage. If she leaves, I'll come and get you."

"*Merci*, Lucas."

Although I wasn't hungry, I ordered a small pizza and a glass of merlot. Expecting the street boys to search for me, I chose a table next to a white picket fence that separated the patio from the walk.

Nearby I heard a familiar voice.

"There she is," said Pierre.

Pierre and Adrien came to the patio, followed by several other boys. "Madame Charlotte, Mademoiselle Shelley is in the Garage! What should we do?"

"Nothing. It's okay. I'm waiting for her."

The waiter deposited the steaming pizza before me and said "go away" to the boys.

Pierre straightened, and a sly grin crossed his face. "Ohh," he said, inhaling the aroma. He raised his eyebrows three or four times rapidly, cocked his head, pouted with a protruding bottom lip and whined, "Madame Charlotte, I'm hongry."

"Do you want a pizza, Pierre?"

"Not now, Pierre," interrupted Adrien. "The music's starting." He pulled on Pierre's arm and said, "Later, Madame Charlotte, later, okay?"

The sounds of Sweet Mickey's band, Boukman Eksperyans, boomed over the entire block. Even trees swayed in the breeze to his Haitian rhythms.

I had just taken a piece of pizza when Henri and several older boys appeared. "Madame Charlotte, Mademoiselle Shelley is--"

"I know. It's okay."

"Have a good evening, Madame. *Bon soir.*"

"*Bon soir.*"

My pizza was finished when Pierre and Adrien re-appeared.

"Now?" asked Pierre, his head nodding up and down.

"How many are you?"

"A lot," laughed Adrien.

"Fourteen," added Pierre.

I waved to the waiter.

"Two pizzas to go, please, cut into fourteen pieces."

"Fourteen, Madame?"

"Yes, fourteen."

He hesitated, looked at the boys and said austerely, "As you wish."

"Thank you, Mama, thank you," said Adrien.

"I'm not Mama. I'm *grunmoun*, remember?"

Pierre slapped his thigh.

Surrounded by salivating boys, Pierre carried the box. He glanced over his shoulder and grinned like the man in the moon who found green cheese.

While Shelley said goodnight to her friends, I strolled ahead and leaned against a tree, waiting.

A wire of bare light bulbs swayed, illuminating tropical foliage. Men in dress slacks and women in satins stood in small groups talking. Gold jewelry flashed as the light swung toward them. A visual night lullaby.

Shelley was walking toward me when she heard her name called.

"Mademoiselle Shel-lee. Mademoiselle Shel-lee!"

She stopped and turned to see Garry Jean, a street boy of

ten years of age, standing in the middle of street. I saw him, too, a slight figure with bony knees twirling a green fluorescent strand.

Saying nothing, she looked at him, and he made no move toward her.

"I love you!" he called loudly. "And I love your mother, too."

Shelley watched him disappear, then continued toward me, her head down. She wiped her cheeks before she reached me. I draped my arm around her neck, pulled her over, and kissed her on the forehead.

For Christmas, my college son, Jon, arrived. On a scheduled flight to the Central Plateau, Jon joined us on the small plane. The pilot graciously went further north to circle the *Citadelle*, a massive fortress that sits on a mountain top. Built by King Henri Christophe, it opened in 1820 and is a proud national monument.

The Citadelle, *largest fortress in Western Hemisphere*

December 1993 Christmas Eve Dinner at the Hotel Villa

Christmas cards arrived with good wishes. One card

contained a check for five hundred dollars. I read and re-read the handwritten note.

"Haiti's need is so great, and Helen and I recount our blessings. Enclosed is $500 for you to do with as you see fit for a greater need. Best wishes, Art."

Praising God, my heart leaped. At last.

Shelley and I spent considerable time choosing the boys who would most likely benefit.

"What school do you want to attend?" I asked Pierre and Adrien.

"But Madame, what do we do about uniforms?" asked Adrien.

Thinking aloud, I said, "I know a school. Their uniform is white shirt and brown slacks."

Pierre grinned. "Nice *rad* (clothes). And we need shoes."

I hadn't considered the cost or care of uniforms. Where would these boys who were homeless keep their uniforms?

A white shirt? I grimaced.

Adrien leaned closer to add, "Madame, we also have to buy books."

Ka-ching. Ka-ching.

"Can we go?" asked Pierre. His usual mask of mischief was down, and the heart of a boy exposed. "I want to read."

Shelley with her Christmas request, a fancy machete

"We all want to read, Madame Charlotte."

I told them I would visit the headmaster and find out the costs before deciding.

Adrien arched his back and spun one arm in a softball

pitcher's windup. "We want to go to school, but the school may not want us."

True.

The studious headmaster listened as I described the street boys and their desire for education.

With a long fingernail, he scratched his Afro and pushed his horn-rimmed glasses back on the bridge of his nose. The thick lens exaggerated the roundness of his eyes, giving him a constant, inquisitive look.

"Street children? My, my. I don't know. They're children without mamas, you know. I'm uncertain how they would fit in with our students."

"Not many," I said. "With tuition and books, perhaps I can enroll five. In which session do you have fewer students, the morning or afternoon?"

"The afternoon," he said, knitting his brow.

"Can they attend that session?" I pulled out my checkbook. "I'll pay for the entire semester in advance."

With the Haitian economy tanking, many students had dropped out of school because their parents couldn't afford monthly tuition. I calculated that the school needed money to pay salaries.

His magnified eyes focused on my checkbook.

"I'll ensure they have a full, hot meal before they come. Isn't there a Haitian proverb about a hungry belly?"

His broad smile widened his jaws, making his face and oversized glasses more symmetrical.

"Oh, you know," he said in surprise. "A hungry belly has no ears."

"Yes, that's it. The boys need to eat before they come to class." Clearing my throat, I took pen and paper from my purse. "Tuition for five students comes to how much money?"

"That would be fifteen dollars a month for each student for ten months."

I scribbled it down.

"And the cost of books?"

His eyes never left my checkbook as he estimated another fifteen dollars per student for the year.

I tried mentally to convert the tuition for five boys for ten months from Haitian dollars into Haitian gourdes, add the amount for books and for money for a full, five-gourde meal every day for the boys, but it was too much for me. I was as tangled as a kitten in a mess of yarn.

I decided to deal with books and food later and pay the tuition to reserve the seats.

"Now about uniforms. You know, these children don't have a place to keep a uniform or the means to keep it clean. Is it possible that since they're from the street, you might forego the rule for uniforms for them?"

His smile vanished.

"Of course, I can buy uniforms," I quickly added, "but I don't think you want the boys seen in Petionville in dirty uniforms."

"No, of course not," he scoffed, "that would reflect poorly on the school."

"The boys can start right away, just as soon as you approve. I can pay today." I re-examined my tuition calculations and was satisfied my estimate could pay for six boys.

The headmaster stretched his arms to relax the fit of his jacket sleeves. With elaborate gestures, he selected a clean piece of paper and a pen.

Stretching his arms again, he prepared to write. "What are their names?"

"Pierre, Adrien, Lucas, Nicolas, Rafel and Garry Jean."

"Their last names?"

"They'll give them to you."

The Haitian grapevine worked quickly, and the remaining boys clamored that they, too, should attend school.

Again, I called upon UNICEF. By then, a chief administrator and I were friendly acquaintances.

"Can't you do something?" I implored.

"It's so sad," she said. "Like I told you, UNICEF funds are restricted. We can fund beds, uniforms, and soaps, but we must give the money to an institution or foundation. We are not prepared to give to children on the streets, and they don't belong to an institution or foundation."

I decided to place five more in school at my expense.

"What about you, Henri?" I asked.

Henri smiled and wagged his head "no."

The twins made the sign of rubbing money between the thumb and fingers. "Henri likes to gamble."

Grinning, Henri pushed one of them.

"Little Boniface should go so he has a good chance."

"What about Noa?"

Adrien whispered, "No, Noa's brother is becoming an *attaché*.

"Don't forget Leon," said Adrien. "He wants to go."

"Leon?"

Holding up his index finger, he made a cutting motion at the first joint.

"Oh yes." The one who lost the tip of his finger to a *marchand's* machete.

After more discussion, a consensus emerged. Shelley and I discussed the prospects, and five more were selected.

I returned to the headmaster who again stretched his arms to loosen his jacket sleeves before taking his paper.

"What are their names?"

CHAPTER TWENTY-ONE

"After the dancing, the drum is heavy."

— HAITIAN PROVERB

In the first days of January, the street boys were strangely absent. On the fourth day, one of the twins, Adrien and Henri waited just inside Presse Evangelique grounds, hidden well behind bushes next to the gate.

With an aura of fear, the three surrounded me and whispered.

"We need your help, Madame Charlotte," said Adrien.

The single twin nervously glanced over his shoulder as the other two spoke.

"Pierre and his brother are missing," said Henri.

The twin said, "My father has gone everywhere, asked everyone. All the *marchands* in the marketplace and on the corners. The business owners. No one talks."

"The *attachés* have them. Find them, please," begged Adrien.

Fidgeting, one whispered "if they're still alive."

"How do you know the *attachés* have them?"

They exchanged glances, debating how much to tell.

I waited.

Henri said, "Because the *attachés* first had only the two twins, not Pierre. But this one cried a lot." He put his arm on the little boy's shoulder. "He said that it was Pierre who took the cell phone in the grocery store, not him."

"They believed him?"

Henri shrugged. "They let him go and took Pierre."

A hard sickness weighted my stomach, like melted metal.

What are their chances of being alive? I wondered. *And if they are, what terrible things have happened? Dear sweet*

Pierre who loves the world and everyone in it. And the little twin."

I felt completely powerless. "I don't know where to begin to look for them."

Adrien's eyes teared. "Please, Madame Charlotte. You have to find them, please."

I thought of the grocery store, the one that catered to internationals. I knew the owner, and we often joked with one another. I decided to ask him for help.

"Sit here, Madame Charlotte," the owner said, indicating a chair across from his desk. "What can I do for you?"

"Messieur Antoine, two of the street boys have disappeared, taken by *attachés* I'm told. I don't know where to begin searching for them. Do you know anything?"

The well-toned mulatto owner drummed his fingers on his desk. "I've heard," he said. "The father of one of the boys is asking everyone."

"The twin. Initially, both twins were taken. Then one proclaimed his innocence and blamed Pierre, so they released him and took Pierre. They've been missing now for several days, almost a week."

His nostrils flared.

"Can you help?"

Messieur Antoine studied me as though assessing the amount of information I might possess.

He clasped his hands and said, "When the cell phone of a woman disappeared, the husband was totally irate and accused two of the boys. I told him that the boys may not have taken it."

"What happened?"

"His wife was at the cashier when she noticed her cell phone missing. Since the boys were in the store at the time, she told her husband the boys had stolen it. He took revenge."

"And he's an *attaché*," I added quietly.

"I don't know about that," he said, looking away and reaching for the phone.

Of course, he knows.

Messieur Antoine spoke too quickly in Haitian Kreyol for me to comprehend, but his commands were clear. His rapid baritone reverberated, as though rebounding off rusted metal in a barrel. Each harsh syllable pummeled flakes of rust.

CHAPTER 21 | 253

I grasped the question, "Where are the boys?"

At the answer, Messieur Antoine lacerated the person on the receiving end. His eyes narrowed as he snapped questions. When the other person spoke, he was silent. His fist tightened, and his tone harshly accelerated. When he glanced at me, he spoke more rapidly. I understood only my name.

I speculated he berated the man for his absolute stupidity to kidnap these boys when knowledge prevailed that the Americans would still invade. And an American woman sits across from him at this moment.

Messieur Antoine grimaced as the man resisted. In a loud voice, he bellowed a command and slammed the phone down.

I swallowed.

This man has more power than I expected, and he thinks, as an American, I have more power than I do.

"The boys will be released right away," he replied curtly. Then his tone assumed a note of tenderness.

"You look tired, Madame Charlotte."

I half-smiled, nodding.

"You and your daughter should go to our beach resort for a day or two. You work too hard. Relax, enjoy the Caribbean. Call me when you want to go, and I'll make the arrangements."

The missing boys re-appeared, but Pierre wasn't the same. A pervasive melancholy enveloped him. I stroked his cheek. "You'll be all right," I whispered.

"*Merci*, Madame, *merci*," he replied as he mindlessly kicked the tires of my machine.

"Thank Messieur Antoine at the store. He's the one who found you."

He brightened. "He did?"

"Yes," I said, encouragingly. "He knew where to call and find you, and he demanded they release you immediately!"

Pierre beamed. A man of importance had cared enough about him, *timoun nan lari-yo,* Pierre, to find him.

The father of the twins made a special trip to Presse Evangelique. Grasping my hand in both of his and through tears, he stammered his gratitude. As a parent, I could only imagine his pain and relief.

Yet Messieur Antoine was right. I was exhausted, and oddly, it was Victor who showed me. Victor no longer carried a stick, and he often prevented smaller ones from pestering me at night at my machine.

"Madame Charlotte has given to you today," and putting his strong arm on the child's shoulder, he moved him away. Taking my keys, he opened the door and ensured it was locked.

One evening he accompanied me to a medical clinic with a sick boy. "Go home, Madame Charlotte. You're tired. I'll stay with him and tell you tomorrow what's wrong with him."

At home, fatigue stung every fiber of my body. A memory drifted through of someone saying, "You re-nourish other people. Who re-nourishes you?" I needed re-nourishment, and I accepted Messieur Antoine's kind offer for Shelley and me to stay a night at his beach resort.

We arrived at our whitewashed, thatched roof cottage to a decadent greeting bowl of watermelons, cantaloupes, sliced oranges and pineapple topped with mint leaves.

Afterward, I lay in a chaise lounge. With my eyes closed, I rested to the lapping of the Caribbean in a small cove.

Slap, swish. Slap, swish. The cadence hypnotized me. Nearby Shelley swam and then built a sandcastle.

"Mom, are those our battleships out there?"

I sat up, shading my eyes. "It's an American flotilla, probably patrolling for the embargo."

"And for the boatloads of Haitians heading for Miami."

"Yes."

The dinner and evening completely relaxed both of us. In the morning, while Shelley slept soundly, I slipped out to walk on the beach.

High tide had begun receding. The sound of cascading waves soothed me, and I played in wet sand. As I walked toward the far point, the wind picked up. Avoiding rocks, I walked to the fringe of succulent cacti. Then I stopped.

Strewn among the cacti and high sand were household items. A blue plastic kitchen strainer, an orange colander, a white dish rack. Tennis shoes lay scattered. Other household items were caught on bushes and littered the point. A drenched child's doll lay alone.

Perhaps some of the items were from capsized boats, perhaps not, but the doll most probably was. Picking up the doll, I sat down and gazed at the debris of dreams.

Haiti doesn't recognize boundaries or limits. There's always room for one more, whether in a tap-tap, a truck or a boat. Sunk low in the water with the weight of so many, the boats easily tip in surging waves.

I straightened the skirt on the doll and wondered about the little girl whose fate led her to her final moments in a restless ocean rather than a safe sleep on America's shores. I smoothed the doll's hair filled with drying sand and gently laid her among the cacti.

CHAPTER TWENTY-TWO

"A rock in the river doesn't know the agony of a rock in the sunshine."

— *HAITIAN PROVERB*

The difficult times predicted by the Round Table and Craig came to pass in 1994.

Before an evening storm, I stood on my balcony, listening to rumbling thunder and watching jagged lightning approach from the ocean. I remembered another night when green lightning repeatedly struck a single spot in the distant ocean. I wondered if the gates of Hell might look like that.

In the ensuing six months, suffering came, and with it, a

rotting of hope, a poverty of soul. Outside of our home, a woman picked leaves to eat, and frequent wails of grief penetrated every wall. Even now, so many years later, the heaviness of those days pushes my heart into a dark cavern.

In January 1994, flies buzzed around Rafel's face and drank from the sweat on his upper lip as his head tipped in sleep. His shirt open, I stared at his protruding ribcage and the stark, white bandage on his shoulder. The nurse shook her head and handed me an ointment.

"Life is bad in Haiti, Madame Charlotte," she said.

In February, while walking down a street in *la ville*, a tortured mother grabbed me by the arm and thrust a prescription toward me. In her arms, she carried a feverish baby wrapped in blankets. The prescription was for oral re-hydration. Her baby was dying, and she had no money.

"I don't know where a pharmacy is," I said, aching with her desperation.

Pulling me by the arm and clutching her baby, we ran two blocks to a corner store. Her mouth hung open, waiting to scream, as she pushed me toward the rear where a small pharmacy operated.

While I completed the transaction, she moaned and stroked the head of her dying baby, her black eyes wild in fear.

Handing her the medication, I asked, "Do you know--?" But she was gone, running with all of the life in her sinewy body to save her baby.

I cried on the way home, praying God would save the baby, that God would spare Haiti.

Still, the human spirit cannot be suppressed, and life for the street boys continued. Lucas informed me they needed a new soccer ball. In retrospect, I think it was this kind of jocularity that saw me through those days.

When I asked what happened to the old one, Henri said, "It popped."

"Popped?" I looked at their bare feet.

"We kick hard, Madame."

We all knew that I would give in. I might give in for the sake of harmony, or because the argument isn't worth the battle, or because who cares in the long run, or because I have ill-defined boundaries or because I loved them.

"I'll get the ball."

Lots of mixed commotion.

"The thugs said they'll steal it and sell it," whined a little one.

"You can all sign the ball, and I'll register it with the police." I pointed to the station across from the store.

Eyes bulged. Bodies jerked. "The police? But they're part of the *attachés*."

"No matter. When the thugs hear I've gone to the police, they'll leave the ball alone."

What fun to watch them passing the ball from one to another, handing the pen, saying, "your turn." Some signed only their first name; others seriously signed their full name, while others slowly made an exaggerated "X."

After the curlicues were drawn and inspections of signatures, they handed the ball to me. I proudly walked to the police station. Only a few boys found the courage to wait outside.

Two policemen stared as I entered. One stood scratching his head, cap in hand. The other placed his leg on a chair and leaned on his knee.

"I want to register this ball with the police," I announced.

Unimpressed.

"Some thugs are threatening to steal this ball, and it belongs to the street boys. I purchased it for them, and I want to register it. I thrust the ball forward for their examination of the boys' signatures of ownership.

They didn't blink an eye.

"If it's stolen, I will press charges."

They don't know the judicial phrase, I thought. Since a fair justice system is the cornerstone of a democracy, we weren't on the same page.

The one leaning on his propped knee placed his chin in his hand.

"So, it is now understood that if this ball is stolen, I will expect you to arrest the culprits."

Like mannequins, they didn't say a word or even move.

Inwardly, I chuckled. *Arrest the thugs who are connected to the attachés who are the paramilitary secret police, and therefore, an unofficial arm of the police itself.*

Nevertheless, the Haitian grapevine would spread the news that Madame Charlotte, an American, had gone to the police over a soccer ball. The ball would be left to burst in its own time by one bare toe too many.

In late April, Bill and Liz said goodbyes to our Round Table and left for new shores. Both bemoaned, "Ten thousand people out of work this week alone."

When I delivered a pizza to Pierre and friends one night, they fell on it like a pack of starving dogs. I yelled at them and said I would get another pizza, but they must stand in line and take their piece.

I returned with another pizza and asked, "Who will be the leader? The leader will distribute each piece and eat last."

Pierre reluctantly volunteered. The image of him sitting on the curb, literally starving, yet faithfully distributing each piece until all had been served, will stay with me forever.

In April, Shelley and I watched a movie video of DIE HARD on a night of unusual electricity. As the star tiptoed across broken glass silently between machine gun rat-a-tat-tats, a machine gun volley outside our window shattered our silence. The enemy answered in kind again, and then both burst together, firing into the darkness.

Shelley and I stared at each other and at the video, which continued its silent scene.

"That's REAL!" said Shelley, looking toward the window.

"Get down! Stay away from the windows. It's time for us to leave, Shelley."

"When school's out," she insisted.

In May, I lay in darkness, listening to the grinding motor of a large truck descending the ravine. A haunting scream, a shot, followed by another twelve executions.

In early May as expected, all airlines announced that flights in and out of Haiti would cease on June 20th. I booked us on a flight for June 19th.

The police retaliated with increased roadblocks. Since our home lay between two major intersections, we encountered the hostile, payback-time attitude. In addition to producing all papers, we answered lengthy questions.

On a Saturday morning, Shelley and two friends were stopped in two police roadblocks. Separately, I was stopped in another and delayed. When we couldn't locate each other, we neared panic, thinking the other might be in police custody for a minor violation.

That was a deciding moment.

"It's time for you to go, Shelley, right after school's out. I'm booking you on the first flight after June 8th, if I can."

"When are you going?"

"June 19th. I need to prepare the offices so they can still operate while I'm gone."

Shelley fell back in the chair and firmly placed her hands on the arms. "I'm not going."

"Yes, you are if I can get you on a plane. I can't be worrying about you while I'm working. And you can't be worrying about me."

American Airlines had one remaining seat for June 11th.

"Meant for you," I said.

On June 8th, school was out. For dinner, we went to our favorite French restaurant.

"What a year you've had. You've blossomed."

Shelley smiled. "It's been a good year."

"What's the best part?"

"Tennis. Good friends. The Villa. And science. Well, astronomy, not science."

"You're coming into your own. I'm proud of you."

On that same day, the Organization of American States (OAS) issued a resolution condemning Haiti's "massacres, arson, detentions, rapes, summary executions, torture, forced disappearances, and mutilation of corpses."

Many words on paper, like a mass grave, I thought. *We are numb to the quenching of personal breath, the chopping of limbs, the screams of the unwilling, the crying children. Although generic words may censure, there is no face on them. A country's violent upheavals, thousands dead, thousands starving, encapsulated in thirteen words.*

The OAS approved the formation of an invasion force

under the leadership of the United States.

On June 11th, Shelley and I walked in silence through the jammed airport, barely holding hands. Checked in, we approached the immigration entry door.

An unsmiling military officer sat on a stool; his leg outstretched.

I wondered what he thought about these internationals fleeing his country. After the Americans come, his job might be toast, and there goes the bread on his table.

Shelley handed him her papers.

My breath was shallow. Echoes of Liz's warnings returned *"Internationals are being hassled at the airport. Some are being denied exit."*

I looked at the painted, sliding door guarding entry to the immigration area and knew when Shelley walked through that door, I wouldn't be able to see her.

I fought panic.

We clasped hands, and I looked into her bereft face.

"You'll be all right. And I'll be all right. I'll wait right here by this door until I know you've made it through immigration. I'll stay here until I see the plane in the air, so if you need me, I'm here."

The military officer returned Shelley's papers and pushed open the sliding immigration door.

I saw the lines of silent internationals waiting their turn to exit through the immigration aisles.

"I love you," I said.

"I love you, too," she whispered.

We hugged, and tears rolled down my cheeks.

I wiped my eyes and watched Shelley enter and take her place in the line. Then the officer pulled the door closed.

I didn't leave. I stared at the painted door and bit my lips to hold tears that could not be held.

The officer slowly slid open the door with his foot so that I could see my daughter.

"*Merci*," I said.

He pretended not to hear.

Shelley looked back and we waved.

Finally, waving high and forlornly, Shelley passed into the waiting area for departure.

I blew a kiss and waved again.

CHAPTER TWENTY-THREE

"God's pencil has no eraser."

— *HAITIAN PROVERB*

On Sunday morning, June 19, 1994, I joined the crush of fleeing Haitians to board one of the last four planes out of Haiti.

As my staff and I approached the airport entry, I was shocked. "Is that the line to get into the lobby?"

A long line of would-be entrants snaked from the front doors of departure to the front doors of arrivals. Military guards patrolled the area and prevented panic shoving. To enter, I showed my passport and ticket.

Yet inside the jammed airport lobby, Haitian style pushing, shoving, and crowding ruled the day.

Pressing through the crowd, I asked an airline attendant, "Where's the line for the Miami 11:30 flight?"

She directed me toward the rear of the very longest line that extended well beyond the main lobby.

Hauling my army-sized duffle bag, I pushed my way through to the rear of the line. The line made no progress.

I looked at the family behind me and shrugged.

"People cutting in," the father said.

"Where are you going?" I asked.

"New York."

Dumbfounded, I repeated, "New York? Isn't this the line for Miami?"

A man in front of me turned and questioned, "New York? I thought this was Miami."

The father behind me repeated, "New York."

The man in front said, "I'll check. I'm going to Miami."

I sweated in suffocating heat. My throat scratched with dryness. I searched for my water bottle. Realizing I had forgotten it, I hailed a Red Cap, a luggage bearer.

"Can you buy me a Coca-Cola at the machine?"

Of course he could.

I stretched across three children and handed him the money.

While I waited, I pondered what a different attitude I had now than upon arrival. Trust. Without question, I knew the Red Cap would return with my soda and exact change. Amused, I chuckled at the affection I felt.

Sipping my cola slowly, I inched forward.

The investigating passenger returned from his quest and announced, "We're in the wrong line. This is New York. Miami's on the other side."

I looked across a bobbing sea of a black heads.

The crowd pressed so closely I was unable to take three steps with my large duffle bag. I hailed another Red Cap, who struggled to break through the crowd to reach the bag. Finally, he stretched, leaned over a body, and grabbed an edge of fabric, not the handle.

Guaranteed for life, the bag ripped, and my clothing tumbled on the floor. Several bent down, shoved the clothing back into the torn bag, and the Red Cap and I pushed our way through to another airline attendant.

Examining my ticket, she asked, "Are you on the 11:30 flight?"

"Yes."

She examined the ticket again, asked the question again and received the same answer.

"Over there," she said, pointing to a shorter line.

Hope swelled. *I may make the flight yet.*

A woman with children pointed to my torn bag. The mother fished in a diaper bag and produced several diaper pins so that I might pin together critical areas.

The line failed to move.

"Why aren't we moving?" I asked. "It's ten o'clock. We need to be checking in. We still have to go through immigration."

"What flight are you on?" the mother asked.

"Miami, 11:30.

"This is Miami, 2:45. This line won't move until the morning flights are finished at the counter."

Leaving my torn bag, I intercepted an airline attendant standing guard to prevent a surging human tsunami at the counter.

Looking at my ticket, he said, "Your ticket is in error."

I blinked.

"The time says 11:30, but the flight number is for the 2:45 flight."

"Which is it? When I booked, they said it was the morning 11:30 flight. I think that's it."

"The line for the 11:30 is over there." He pointed to a disorderly group of people.

"I can't even see a line there."

"It's there."

I wanted to shout *No one knows what a line is in this forsaken country!*

"I'll miss the flight, and there won't be an available seat on the 2:45."

He jerked away to block an impatient Haitian man intent upon forcing his way to the counter.

"Look. You let that Haitian family go ahead. I saw you. You have your own little line right here." I pointed to the floor where he was standing.

He turned and looked at the Haitian family now embroiled with a ticket counter clerk.

"They have Visas."

"I have a passport. And my government has ordered me out of the country. I need to be on that 11:30 plane."

He shrugged, like it's-not-my-problem.

I took a deep breath, disliking myself for what I was about to do.

Getting in his face, and I mean that literally, right in his face, I argued Haitian style. Vociferously with a scathing tone, I slapped the back of one hand into the palm of the other, and he saw the underside of my pink tongue.

"If I'm not on that plane, I'm going to call CBS, CNN, ABC, NBC, Associated Press, and the President of your company and tell them about the inefficiency (a louder slap of my hands) of the Haitian airline personnel evacuating Americans."

I left out his mother.

He paused, his eyes scanning the ceiling.

"All right. When this family is through, you're next. Stand here."

"I'll get my bag. Merci."

That family, however, was engaged in its own arguments

with the ticket counter clerk. One of their American visas had expired.

I checked my watch. Ten forty-five. Immigration still waited.

When I handed my American passport and ticket to the clerk, I breathed a sigh of relief. While she confirmed I was booked on the morning flight, I helped a baggage attendant tape the rip in my bag with duct tape.

"Where is your passport?" asked the clerk.

"I gave it to you."

"No, you didn't."

"I distinctly recall handing it to you. You must have it here somewhere."

"No, I don't. Look at the lines. If you don't have your passport, I don't have time to help you."

I dumped the contents of my purse and my briefcase. No passport. I searched the floor. No passport. Several attendants took apart the front of the counter. No passport.

My hands began to shake. I would be stranded in the American Embassy.

I wanted to scream. *I just want to go home!*

Leaving my bag, I retraced my steps, leaping over luggage, elbowing my way with everyone else.

No passport.

Two military officers chatted in a far corner. I wondered if they would help me and immediately concluded I must be out of mind. Nevertheless, perhaps the presence of a military officer might jog the clerk's memory.

"Excuse me. I lost my passport at the ticket counter. Can you please help me?"

They were stunned.

Then one broke into a wide smile. "An American passport can never be found. It's worth a lot of money." He rubbed his fingers together.

Exactly what I feared.

I looked at the other officer.

"Please."

"I'll go with you, but look--" He gestured over the waving sea of frantic people. "There's not much hope."

Walking with a tall uniformed military officer, I didn't need to push my way through the crowd. It parted naturally.

As we approached the ticket counter, the clerk immediately

processed the officer. She nonchalantly held up my passport and said, "We found it. Someone turned it in."

"Where was it?"

She pointed to the floor where I was standing, an area I had scoured unsuccessfully.

"Amazing."

In the immigration line, I conversed with the fellow behind me. His travel experience was going very well. He belonged to Haiti's wealthy class, the top one percent of the population that received half of the nation's income in 1991.

Tall, with fair skin, blue eyes, a Greek nose and naturally curly hair, he looked more like a feminine Adonis than a native Haitian.

"The Americans are so boring with their remarks about the MRE'S."

"The Morally Repugnant Elite?"

"It's not a sin to get by," he continued, speaking to the air.

"Ah, *degage pa peche*," I said. "It's not a sin to take care of yourself and your family and friends first, even at the expense of everyone else?"

"Nonsense. The bourgeois are not *amused* with the

political charade." He affectedly emphasized *charade* as *cha-raad*. His fingers traced the shape of, but never touched his curls.

I recalled the Round Table solution to world problems.

If the U.N. had slapped a boycott on all Haitian passports, the crisis would have ended within twenty-four hours! Economic embargos never hurt the rich, only kill the poor. The rich leave or raise their prices.

"Where are you going?" I asked as I bit my tongue to prevent adding, *while the poor in your country are left to eat leaves.*

"I'm off to Paris to study art and painting. Then I'm going to the Amalfi Coast and Egypt, but first, I'm going to stop in London to visit a friend, a young Haitian artist and affirm her worth. She's depressed. I'm going to help her -- what is the English word?"

His hand glided into the unseen horizon.

"Oh, yes, *clouds*. I will help her chase away her clouds."

I was not amused.

Sitting on the plane, waiting for take-off, I leaned back and settled in, silent with prayers of gratitude.

In a row ahead, a corpulent woman berated a man for

having her aisle seat. In her fury, her rear shook, her bosoms heaved, and the net of her vintage hat unrolled.

The man refused to budge.

The woman stomped off to locate the flight attendant.

Faces may change, power brokers may change, but Haiti is Haiti, caught in a time warp and bursting with energy.

Haiti had not changed. I had.

EPILOGUE

"The firefly lights a path for its own eyes."

— HAITIAN PROVERB

On September 19, 1994, the United States troops invaded Haiti in Operation Restore Democracy. The Haitian people hailed them as liberators. They cheered, drew large hearts in colored chalk on the highways, and lined the road, waving hand-sized American flags.

A Haitian proverb says, "*The dew thinks it's big stuff until the sun comes up.*" American tanks bulldozed the headquarters of FRAPH, organization of the paramilitary.

However, the disbanded military and *attachés* melted into

the general population or disappeared in the Artibonite mountains to fight another day.

In Haiti, there is always another day.

US posters dropped in rural areas say soldiers are here to help you when they come

US posters dropped in rural areas say soldiers are here to help you when they come

THE ECHO PROGRAM

(THE EMERGENCY CHILDREN'S HEALTH OPERATION)

Canada funded the Emergency Children's Health Operation (ECHO) with $100,000. The food program would feed 3,000 children under the age of four and their mothers on the Central Plateau. Under Lisette's guidance as Coordinator for Mother-Child Health, our staff organized the remote villages. They chose a community center or someone's home as the central meeting place where they would cook food and have their nutritional lessons.

My Canadian assistant questioned my decision to purchase the foodstuffs in downtown Port-au-Prince before we had a way to deliver. No trucks were available for the dangerous drive. Small planes had ceased flying. The situation appeared hopeless. In answer to prayers, I felt the urge to proceed.

My answer to him was one my childhood pastor often quoted. "If you pray for rain, carry an umbrella." I went on to say, "This is a calculated risk. We must be ready, and we must trust."

I purchased thousands of dollars of food stuffs with an agreement that the food would be held for us in a local truck. Therefore, when needed, I only had to call.

There are no coincidences. In a back-country restaurant, I ran into three U.S. Special Forces soldiers. They suggested I contact a particular Colonel in Port-au-Prince, with no precise location.

Meanwhile, I had observed casually dressed men meeting at the Hotel Villa Creole at the Sunday Brunch. When one such meeting was adjourned, I approached the lone gentleman who remained sitting at the head of the table.

Brigadier General Bruce Bingham was in command of civil operations in Haiti. After I submitted a letter with details, he arranged for a scheduled Blackhawk helicopter on route to Hinche to transport our foodstuffs in a cargo net.

At the tiny grass airport near Pignon, U.S. Army jeeps armed with machine guns arrived to meet the helicopter.

Hundreds of our Haitian farmers, armed with machetes, surrounded the area, and took possession of its precious cargo.

Much later, standing on mustard earth in a remote village, I marveled at steaming, black caldrons emitting mouth-watering aromas.

Woman in remote area

Nearby, in a thatched community hut, women with suckling infants recited their nutrition lesson in rhythmic cadence. I listened to chants that filled me with a deep sense of accomplishment and closure.

Toddler by village cauldron

Remote Haitian hut

"What do we need to eat today?"

"We need beans and rice and vegetables."

Nude toddlers scampered in the yellow dust around the thatched hut. Each child had grown an inch of rich, black hair roots, contrasting sharply with the brittle, red hair remaining above. No more red hair of kwashiorkor or swollen bellies.

Lisette, the Haitian Coordinator for Mother-Child Health, squeezed my hand and introduced me as the woman who had provided this program. Their sincere applause brought us to tears.

I've often wondered if this is what God had in mind when He sent me to Haiti. Surveys from my organization said that no child died through that period, and the people attributed that amazing fact to this food program.

Or did God send me to Haiti to provide for the street boys during times of starvation and injury? To rescue them on that dreadful designated day of assassination.

Or did God send me to Haiti to rescue Shelley? And to rescue me?

Frankly, I don't know the answer. Perhaps there is more than one purpose. Perhaps life is as simple as "Do the right thing," or as Mary said, "Do what God puts on your heart."

In December 1999, Shelley and I returned to Haiti for a

brief visit. I arrived first. The joyful reunions with the street boys were as though little time had passed. After all, they live in the present moment.

Pierre had become associated with the Assembly of God Church. He arrived at our reunion dancing, jumping up and down as he had done with the Queen of Sheba tarp, scrubbed, and dressed in his Sunday best. Forever mischievous, he took pleasure in putting his arm around *la belle*, "Mademoiselle Shelley."

Henri begged me to take his new baby home to America. He was involved in questionable activities, possibly running drugs and/or carrying money. A month later, Henri was murdered on a dark street in the middle of the night.

When Lucas drew the attention of a U.S. soldier that a thug had a gun, the soldier arrested the thug. Unfortunately, he failed to handcuff him. The thug picked up a rock and smashed Lucas in the head.

Diagnosed to decline to a vegetable state without surgery, I admitted him to a hospital where a surgeon-friend and another surgeon operated. It was a lengthy operation. My friend refused payment. Lucas survived, and my small church group helped pay expenses.

Adrien retained his innocent nature and insisted upon calling me "Mama." Enrolled in school, his tuition monies gone, I visited his teachers and principal and paid for the rest of the year.

Rafel was in prison.

One had died with leprosy.

Several older ones asked to purchase tools or learn a vocation. Others asked to go to school. I trust they made good use of those opportunities.

Baptiste, my friend and tutor, lives in Miami.

Shelley, my beloved daughter, beats her own drum and treasures its sound. She is an Assistant Professor of Astrophysics at the University of California, San Diego. She builds next generation telescopes and works with Japan on building the camera for the Thirty Meter Telescope, projected to be the largest on earth. She continues to be a popular speaker for SETI and creates instruments for them.

When I recall those moments in the Principal's office and our worry about her promotion to the ninth grade, I smile. And what of the "coincidence" of the new Canadian science teacher who sparked Shelley's pursuit of astronomy? I love God's interventions with perfect timing.

Before Shelley arrived that Christmas of 1999, I sat alone in the restaurant of the Hotel Villa Creole, sipping a glass of wine. Nostalgia assailed me at the speed of light, and each memory brought its own image and emotion.

The glistening swimming pool with a misguided bat and frantic employees.

The Round Table now dispersed.

Pink linen-clad tables on the brick terrace for Sunday brunch.

An abundant rose bougainvillea climbing a white trellis, fulfilling a promising to the roof.

My favorite waiter with a limp calling, "Madame Charlotte, here's a table for you."

Twirling my crystal goblet by the shimmering candle, I followed the illuminating flow through the golden liquid.

There are lights in the darkness if we look for them, but we each must find our path.

THE END

L'HISTOIRE:

"Haiti is slippery ground."

— HAITIAN PROVERB

Haiti and the Dominican Republic share the same island, with Haiti occupying the western one-third. In 1492 Christopher Columbus claimed the entire island for Spain, and its name became Hispaniola.

In their obsessive search for riches, Spanish colonists proceeded to kill most of the indigenous Taino Indians, and disease took the rest. The Taino Indians were a subgroup of the Arawak tribes. They gave the name Haiti, or Ayiti, to the entire island, meaning "land of high mountains."

France obtained the western one-third of the island through French pirates who operated from the small island of Tortuga that lies northwest of Haiti. Preying on Spanish commerce, they lived on and occupied the western section.

In 1697, Spain officially ceded that territory to France, and the French re-named that section Saint-Dominique. With the wealth of their sugarcane plantations, French colonists established a cultural hub and art center.

As a French colony, Saint-Dominique was termed the "Pearl of the Antilles," not surprising since its mountains were rich with mahogany and its fields ripe with sugar. By the end of the eighteenth century, 60,000 whites and freedmen supervised nearly 500,000 slaves.

Yet this was the cruelest of colonies, for the French worked their slaves to death. The average life of the African slave imported from Guinea to Haiti was four years. Their happiness and hope lay in their African spiritual heritage of *Vodou,* which remained the center of their slave community.

In those early years, French planters claimed Haitian mistresses, and those mistresses bore saffron children. Since the French planters did not want their offspring to share the dismal fate of the ebony field laborer, they constructed an economic system that favored their mulatto progeny.

The mulatto progeny became the merchant class. While they did not share the full privileges of free Frenchmen, they still enjoyed more rank and privileges than their darker brothers. The seeds of class and color war were sown.

A slave and *Vodou* priest (*hougan*) named Boukman led a murderous revolt against the French planters in August 1792, heralding the coming Haitian Revolution. It is estimated that 1800 plantations were destroyed, and 1000 slaveholders killed. Boukman is inked in blood in Haitian history.

Horrified, the French commission abolished slavery in Saint-Dominique. However the unwilling, angry French planters appealed to the British. Since the British were at war with France, they willingly occupied the lucrative colony for five years. Of course, slavery was a condition for the occupation.

The sly French countered this move by ending slavery in all French colonies. The idea was to promote a rebellion against the British. The plan worked through the genius of Toussaint L'Ouverture.

A former slave, Toussaint had risen to the rank of General in the Spanish army in Santo Domingo (now the capital of the Dominican Republic). In 1794, with 4,000 black troops, Toussaint invaded his homeland of Saint-Dominique, allegedly on Spain's behalf to reclaim the wealthy colony.

Once there, however, Toussaint deserted the Spanish flag and led a successful rebellion against the British. His greatest ally was yellow fever.

Meanwhile, Napoleon saw an opportunity to restore French prestige and profit by restoring slavery. He sent 20,000 troops to reclaim the "Pearl of the Antilles."

Toussaint fought brilliantly and earned the nickname "L'Ouverture," referring to his uncanny talent for locating weak openings in enemy lines. The nickname became his surname. During this time, he also fought the War of the Knives, a class war between the mulattos and the blacks.

Eventually, Toussaint defeated the mulattoes and reached an agreement with the French whereby the 1801 autonomous Constitution paid homage to France, but Toussaint would be named Governor-General for Life. For his part in the peace, Toussaint was to be permitted to retire on an estate in his beloved homeland.

But politics are fickle, and promises are quickly forgotten. In 1802, when French troops suffered an epidemic of yellow fever and continued defeats at the hands of Haitian revolutionists, the French tricked Toussaint by inviting him to a parley. There, he was seized and shipped to France where he died of pneumonia in a French prison in 1803.

Nevertheless, under Toussaint's lieutenant, Jean-Jacques Dessalines, the Haitian Revolution continued. The French withdrew from Saint-Dominique in December 1803, and a formal Independence Act was signed on January 1, 1804.

Dessalines became the recognized ruler. He resurrected the Taino Indian name for the new country, Ayiti, or Haiti.

Forty years after independence, extensive land reforms were implemented. The reforms abolished most of the lucrative sugarcane plantations, and the land was divided into small acreages, which offered subsistence farming. With the land reforms, the productive sugar economy was lost.

Thus, Haiti came into being, approximately the size of the state of Maryland with 10,640 square miles, as the first black republic in the Western Hemisphere. War-ravaged, a decimated economic base, an illiterate population, inexperienced government leaders, class hatreds, and a history of servitude, Haiti's prospects for success appeared bleak. Worse, their leaders received no help from the developed nations.

Fearing a free slave neighbor might inspire their own slaves to revolt in the South, the United States not only ignored Haiti, it did recognize it as a free country until July 1862. Therefore, the infant country was left to its own devices of structuring a socio-economic-political foundation.

The little republic struggled. Between 1911-1915, it is estimated seven Presidents were assassinated or ousted from power. The instability led the United States government to fear foreign control would result. In fact, both France and Germany were active in Haiti, notably Germany. Of particular concern was the possibility of a foreign power establishing a deep-water port.

An assassination in 1915 of the President led to anarchy, and the United States Marines invaded Haiti. They built the grass airway outside of Pignon. The occupation led to building roads and ensuring the safety of banks, but did nothing to plant seeds for democracy, promote literacy or form a stable system of government.

[Note: *For more about the United States' occupation, refer to https://history.state.gov/milestones/1914-1920/haiti]*

Haiti endured turmoil until 1957 when Doctor Francois Duvalier assumed the Presidency. Francois Duvalier was a black country doctor who gained fame for his campaign to eliminate yaws, a contagious disease found in tropical countries.

After he won the election, he soon appointed himself President-for-Life and became known as "Papa Doc". Later, he amended the Constitution to permit him to name his own successor and to lower the age requirement for the office of President.

"Papa Doc" Duvalier ruled Haiti with an iron hand from 1957 until his death in 1971. In contrast with previous rulers who concentrated their power in the cities with military backing, "Papa Doc" consolidated his power over the entire country. He accomplished this feat by integrating *Vodou* into his political rule.

In order to control the country, "Papa Doc" needed to offset the power of the mulattoes and the military. To do this, he developed a policy of "negritude." He cultivated the *houngans*, male priests of Vodou in outlying provinces. From this group, he formed the infamous Tonton Macoute, a brutal unit within the Haitian paramilitary. Tonton Macoute translates to "Uncle Gunnysack" or "bogeyman," and they lived up to the name. In a child's myth, Uncle Gunnysack captured naughty children in a gunnysack and ate them for breakfast.

This secret police force committed terror and murder, often

making midnight calls upon the elite. It's important to note that "Papa Doc" was dark-skinned, and generally speaking, the dark-skinned majority were considered lesser than mulattos and elites. Dark "Papa Doc" preached national unity and "negritude." He introduced many black leaders into government bureaus, and a black elite flourished. Unfortunately, he did little to care for the needs of the poor, and foreign aid money found its way to his coffers.

In 1963 President Kennedy suspended U.S. aid to Haiti because of brutal repression. In 1974, after "Papa Doc" died, his nineteen-year-old son, Jean-Claude Duvalier, succeeded him as President. U.S. foreign aid resumed.

However, "Baby Doc" was not up to his father's style. He bled the treasury and the Duvalier dynasty monies, allegedly $900 million. He fled to France in 1986 with his high-maintenance wife, who loved fur coats, literally hundreds of them.

The Tonton Macoute were outlawed. Actually, many just went underground; other paramilitary organizations formed. Other leaders came and went until a freak election in 1991.

Under the watchful eye of OAS observers, a free election actually occurred, and the black masses elected Father Aristide, a Catholic priest, as President. Father Aristide preached "liberation theology," which holds that the poor have a right to share in the country's resources. His outspoken criticisms resulted in numerous assassination attempts, and he credited the street boys for saving him on one occasion. In fact, he founded several orphanages for the street children, and in the *coup* of 1991, the paramilitary burned one down.

An exceedingly brutal paramilitary organization formed, and their participants were known as *attachés*. Although they had been operating for some time, they formally organized in 1993, as FRAPH, the Front for the Advancement and Progress of Haiti. This occurred as I arrived. They even had offices in Miami, New York, and Montreal.

Prior to the 1991 election, the paramilitary had been killing Aristide supporters. When Aristide was elected, the paramilitary went into defiance. Most of Aristide's supporters resided in poorer areas, notably in *Cite Soleil*, the worst slum in the Western Hemisphere. Other supporters were farmers and workers in the province. The paramilitary began hunting.

In the Haitian way, Father (now President) Aristide's supporters sought revenge upon those who had murdered, tortured and "necklaced" their friends. "Necklacing" is one form of Haitian revenge for political enemies. A tire is placed around the victim's neck and set on fire.

Some say President Aristide's talks on the radio prompted the violence. A friend confided that while driving his car, he heard President Aristide give a talk, implying that his reforms were being stonewalled and the people knew who their enemies were. Therefore, they knew what to do. Braking, my friend thought, "What's he saying? There will be a *coup d'etat*."

In fact, the military *coup d'etat* occurred shortly after that speech. Venezuela offered Aristide asylum, and a U.S. representative escorted him to the waiting plane.

Lt. General Cedras assumed power, and most believe that Michel Francois, Chief of Police, shared that power. It is alleged that the paramilitary, including FRAPH, was connected with Francois, who had dubbed himself with the title of Colonel.

But Aristide did not go quietly. Political trends supported pro-human rights, pro-democracy, and free elections. Legally elected in the first democratic election in Haiti's history, Aristide exerted pressure in the public forum, from Venezuela to France to the United Nations.

President George Bush, Sr., yielded with a token embargo on selected goods. Many American factories closed. Although goods were not supposed to flow to Haiti, they did. Commerce still flourished with higher prices.

Inflation occurred, and the poor suffered. The economic embargo failed because General Cedras did not resign from power. Pressures mounted for his resignation, and violence escalated. This was the precise timing of my arrival.

The United Nations imposed an oil and guns embargo, accompanying the U.S. embargo on goods, two weeks after my arrival. FRAPH and its *attachés* went into full revenge. The paramilitary rode standing in the beds of white pick-up trucks, carrying rifles. City lights would go dark, and the trucks of marauders made their night killing rounds, eliminating Aristide supporters.

The following two years saw murders, machine-gun fights, butchery, starvation, and cruelness beyond imagination. It worsened as time passed before the invasion.

Ironically, the paramilitary smuggled oil into the country, primarily from the Dominican Republic, and made a fortune. Another irony, attributed to the Round Table, is that cement was exempted from the embargo, and the wife of General Cedras and the Chief of Police, Colonel Francois, owned the largest franchise for cement. The Round Table guffawed at this. The oil smuggling and the cement exemption ensured the Haitian stall tactics would continue because they were making so much money.

Since General Cedras disavowed the Accords for the transfer of power, the U.S. announced it would lead a United Nations' invasion to restore President Aristide to power. Former President Carter and General Powell arrived to negotiate the departure of General Cedras and cronies. The terms, acclaimed by the U.S., were ludicrous to the Round Table.

Haitians, well known for their effective dramas, would have been proud of General Cedras's wife. Hysterical, she claimed she could not leave the country or her home and said something to the extent that she would die first. This brought amusing laughter to our Round Table since the family was celebrating her young son's birthday near that very day.

Next, the U.S. had to promise not to allow their homes to be destroyed, also a common practice among poorer people when the wealthy leave. They take everything, including toilets and sinks. The American negotiating team agreed to rent three homes and lift all sanctions on assets. Finally, General Cedras secured protection and expenses for their large entourage to leave and live in Panama. Millions of U.S. dollars paid.

Note: *one source for this information and reaction is*

https://www.latimes.com/archives/la-xpm-1994-10-14-mn-50281-story.html

How unnecessary. So many concessions over fear of unrest. The unrest had already occurred during the prior two years with the paramilitary war against Aristide supporters. The Haitian people wanted the Americans to intervene. Unfortunately, the negotiators failed to grasp Haiti.

Toward the end prior to evacuation, I bumped into Colonel Francois, the soon-to-be-gone Chief of Police. We were leaving the Hotel Villa Creole at the same time.

He asked, "Where are you going, Madame Charlotte?"

"Maybe Miami, maybe the Dominican Republic." I paused, smiling mischievously, and said, "Where are you going, Colonel Francois?"

He grinned. "Probably the Dominican."

The U.S. and Canada worked together to dismantle Haiti's military and the police. The paramilitary faded into the mountains or formed gangs. U.S. forces bulldozed the headquarters of FRAPH.

Since those years, President Aristide has come and gone. Haiti remains adrift. Often, promised monies are frozen because Haitian leaders refuse to comply with specified requirements. Violent criminal gangs, called *zanglodo*, operate freely, and rumor implies the (new) Haitian National Police are connected.

It appears the country may be less safe now than in 1994. The persistent question lingers, "Why does Haiti remain the poorest country in the Western Hemisphere?"

It's complicated.

THE CONFLUENCE

"Degaje pa peche." "To get by is not a sin."

— *HAITIAN PROVERB*

Cambridge dictionary defines *confluence* as "the place where two rivers flow together and become one larger river; or a situation in which 2 things join or come together."

When Haiti became independent in 1804, the leaders had no notion of how to build institutions that could govern the body politic. They had just come out of slavery, and slavery carries its own master-slave structure. In other words, they yearned for freedom, but lacked the knowledge of the necessary underpinnings.

In the master-slave society, orders of the boss and the pecking order govern the day. For the master, the goal is maximum production with the least cost. For the slave, the goal is survival of the fittest. Individual equality for all does not exist.

Insert the second river, the spiritual beliefs of *Vodou*, and the issues of governance are exacerbated.

A democracy presupposes there are sufficient resources for all. It presupposes that the rule of law will ensure justice and recourse, oblivious to color or social status, and the law will provide order and continuity through institutions, not individuals.

A slave society with spiritual ties to *Vodou* presupposes shifting fortunes and limited resources. Therefore, one should get all one can when one can. It presupposes a whimsy of fate controlled by the spirits, or *loas*. The spirits (deities) are considered intermediaries between *Bondye* (Creator God) and human beings.

In daily life, this translates that if a person has an opportunity for gain, then the *loas* or spirits have placed that advantage for the clever person to seize. Many people place locks on cupboards because Haitian workers might take items. They would not consider it stealing; rather, the spirits or gods had left it for them.

With capricious *loas* also comes the reversal of fortunes, so one must be safe. Avoid becoming involved. Do not speak up or talk because one is here today, gone tomorrow, in power today, ousted tomorrow. Haitian proverbs are peppered with admonitions to be cautious.

May I add, there is sound reason for that. The tragic consequence of these beliefs is that when the gods provide an advantage, it is imperative to take that advantage, to use it to the full extent possible for the benefit of that individual, his family and close friends. Why? Because those advantages may disappear. That is the meaning of *degaje pa peche*; it is not a sin to take care of yourself.

A Haitian proverb says, *"Every government position is papa's horse."* Papa's horse can be anything from siphoning money to a hundred fur coats. The point is the chosen behaviors are for personal gain, not for the body politic.

Consequently, the *Vodou* belief system fosters suspicion and distrust of others in a world of limited resources. It expects abuse of power and stolen advantage. The assumption is there is not going to be enough for everybody, so I must get mine when I have the chance. There is a fear of being taken advantage of, fear of reprisals. These attitudes work against an idea of national unity.

When the U.S. Marines landed in Haiti in September 1994, a common expression was "the Americans are coming to fix everything."

Of course, that is impossible, and when "things" are not fixed, the same problems occur. The failed rescuer becomes culpable. Heroes cheered yesterday may be blamed tomorrow, for ultimately, Haiti is asking to be rescued from itself.

Is there a solution?

Every illiterate person I met expressed a yearning to read. Each of the street boys, from Pierre to Victor, had a burning desire for education. Yet those in power do not value education, except for their own children. Equally disturbing is they fear an educated populace.

During 1994 prior to the American invasion, our organization had to close our adult literacy programs. They became too dangerous to hold. It is an often-ignored fact that when people become literate, they begin to hold leaders accountable. The United Nations found that with the education of girls came a drop in overcrowded populations. In my opinion, reading is the first lynchpin on the path to forming a viable democracy and improved economy.

Yet any financial programs or assistance must hold the

Haitian counterparts accountable. This observation is in bold and underscored. Structured oversight and enforced accounting methods must be thorough. Evaluation efforts must be spelled out and executed. In my time as Director, I can say that enforcing good accounting measures was the toughest task I faced, and I fired people in order to accomplish it.

Often, many inquired about the religious distribution of faiths. Below is a table entitled *"Haiti 2018 International Religious Freedom Report,"* published by the U.S. State Department.

Affiliation	%	Total %
Catholic		55
Protestant		29
Baptist	15	
Pentecostal	8	
Adventist	3	
Methodist	1.5	
Other	0.7	
Vodou *		2.1
Other		4.6
None		10

*Estimates project 50-80% of population practice some form of Vodou.

Many American denominations are active in Haiti, often building churches in the countryside. I would urge them to build schools as well and establish good reporting.

I believe that with reading, education and accountability, Haiti gradually can progress to a state of national unity, one with less whimsy, less fear and, please God, more peace.

ACKNOWLEDGMENTS

My gratitude overflows. My children and grandchildren have steadfastly supported me. My daughter, Shelley Wright, lived in Haiti with me for the first year. Most likely, her perceptions are different, and most certainly, she has her own story. My sons, Stephen and Jon, cheered me on with laughter and love. My artist granddaughter, Melia Wright, created the Map of Haiti. Like her sister, Shannon, and her brother, Conner, she insisted I finish the book.

I am indebted to La Presse Evangelique for their language classes and to my tutor, Baptiste. While the chosen proverbs are found in many countries, in Haiti, proverbs are embedded in the common culture and referenced in daily life. Variations occur, but the meaning is the similar.

My selections came from friends, from online searches, and from *Parol Granmoun* by Edner A. Jeanty and O. Carl Brown, Editions Learning Center, Port-au-Prince, Haiti, 1976.

Special appreciation goes to Jackie Semar, a close friend of many years and my succinct go-to editor. I trust her advice implicitly. For unceasing encouragement and cherished friendship, I thank Cheryl Edwards, Weymuth Heuiser Reed, Ann Sisson Brandes, and my sister, Shirley Burt.

Foremost, I'm grateful to the Christian Reformed World Relief Committee (CRWRC, now "World Renew") and its then International Director, Gary Nederveld, who always supported me through the Haitian crisis. A special shout-out goes to Ron Polinder for his encouragement.

Dr. David and Bonnie Andrew and my good friend, Beverly, sent boxes of clothing for the street boys. My mother's Sunday School class at Grace Baptist Church in Lompoc, California, assembled Christmas pouches. Art and Helen of Mt. Vernon, Washington, graciously sent funds that enabled the street boys to attend school. A special thank you to Merilonne, a former Haitian staff member, who wanted to expand and create programs for street children. Merilonne, I wish we had.

And, of course, to all the street boys. May God be with

you. Finally, my four-second prayer for all street children everywhere, "May God bless you, protect you and guide you throughout your lives."

ABOUT THE AUTHOR

CHARLOTTE ONEILLE ADAMS authors works of historical fiction and political significance. She writes about ordinary people whose lives are upended in pivotal moments, and life-changing decisions must be made. Charlotte holds a graduate degree in political science from the University of California at Berkeley. She lives in San Diego, California. Visit her online at www.CharlotteAdamsAuthor.com

www.ingramcontent.com/pod-product-compliance
Lightning Source LLC
Chambersburg PA
CBHW050301010526
44108CB00040B/1946